REVISE EDEXCEL GCSE (9–1)

History

ANGLO-SAXON AND NORMAN ENGLAND, c1060–88

REVISION
GUIDE AND WORKBOOK

Series Consultant: Harry Smith

Author: Rob Bircher

A note from the publisher

In order to ensure that this resource offers high-quality support for the associated Pearson qualification, it has been through a review process by the awarding body. This process confirms that this resource fully covers the teaching and learning content of the specification or part of a specification at which it is aimed. It also confirms that it demonstrates an appropriate balance between the development of subject skills, knowledge and understanding, in addition to preparation for assessment.

Endorsement does not cover any guidance on assessment activities or processes (e.g. practice questions or advice on how to answer assessment questions), included in the resource nor does it prescribe any particular approach to the teaching or delivery of a related course.

While the publishers have made every attempt to ensure that advice on the qualification and its assessment is accurate, the official specification and associated assessment guidance materials are the only authoritative source of information and should always be referred to for definitive guidance.

Pearson examiners have not contributed to any sections in this resource relevant to examination papers for which they have responsibility.

Examiners will not use endorsed resources as a source of material for any assessment set by Pearson.

Endorsement of a resource does not mean that the resource is required to achieve this Pearson qualification, nor does it mean that it is the only suitable material available to support the qualification, and any resource lists produced by the awarding body shall include this and other appropriate resources.

Contents

· ·

A small bit of small print

Edexcel publishes Sample Assessment Material and the Specification on its website. This is the official content and this book should be used in conjunction with it. The questions in *Now try this* have been written to help you practise every topic in the book. Remember: the real exam questions may not look like this.

The king and the earls

In Anglo-Saxon England it was the king who was the most powerful person in the land: no one could tell the king what to do. In order to govern the country, kings granted out some of their power to their earls and took advice from their council, the Witan.

Law-making
Only the king made new laws, and everyone had to obey them.

The king ruled over all of England, with all its resources at his command.

Landownership
The king could grant land to loyal followers, or take it away in punishment.

Money
The king controlled the minting and distribution of coins.

Powers of the king

Taxation
The king decided when a tax was paid and how much it should be.

Religion
The king was chosen by God to lead his people.

Fyrd
The king could raise the fyrd army and fleet.

Half the country was Anglo-Danish, with its own laws and customs, known as the Danelaw. The king was still king here, but he needed to allow the Danelaw some independence.

The Witan

The Witan was a council that advised the king, but it was not a limitation on the king's power.

- The king decided who was appointed to the Witan.
- The king decided what the Witan should advise him on.
- The king did not have to follow the Witan's advice if he did not wish to.

Thegns (local lords) could complain to the king about earls who governed an earldom badly. This happened with Tostig, the earl of Northumbria in 1065, where the Witan was also involved in deciding what should happen.

The earls

The earls were the most important men in the country after the king and governed large areas of England on the king's behalf. To do this they were granted some of the king's powers:

- ✓ Collecting taxes from their earldom for the king. Earls kept a third of the taxes for governing and protecting their earldom.
- ✓ Overseeing law and order in their earldom. Judging cases and deciding punishments for those found guilty.
- ✓ Military powers. Earls were the king's 'generals', leading their loyal thegns in battle against the king's enemies.

Large earldoms meant earls could become very powerful indeed in Anglo-Saxon England.

Edward the Confessor (1003–66)

Advantages
- 👍 As a religious leader people believed that God was guiding him.
- 👍 He was respected as a wise lawmaker.
- 👍 He was married to Edith, daughter of the rich and powerful Earl of Godwin.

Edward the Confessor in the Bayeux Tapestry.

Disadvantages
- 👎 He had been exiled in Normandy for most of his life, so had few supporters in England.
- 👎 He had no children to succeed him.
- 👎 He struggled to keep control of Earl Godwin.

Now try this

Pick **two** features of the Anglo-Saxon monarchy from the diagram at the top of this page. For each feature, describe how they made the king of Anglo-Saxon England powerful.

Local government and law

Anglo-Saxon England had a complicated system of government that made sure the king's wishes were carried out throughout his kingdom, and that each community completed its duties, especially providing men for the fyrd, collecting tax payments and maintaining law and order.

The shire reeve (sheriff)

The shire reeve was the king's representative in local government.

The king issued orders to the shire reeve through **writs**.

The geld tax was the tax levied on land. Edward the Confessor only levied the tax rarely: he lived on the revenues from his own lands.

Writ from King Edward to his shire reeve

Your responsibilities are:

- To collect revenues from my land in the shire

- To collect the geld tax from the shire when I decide to levy the tax

- To collect fines from the shire court

- To judge cases and witness my laws being enforced at the shire court

- To make sure men are provided for the fyrd and that all roads and defences are well-maintained.

The shire reeve judged at the **shire** court.

The shire reeve was responsible for the defences of the shire.

Shires, hundreds, tithings and hides

☑ Each earldom was divided into shires.

☑ Each shire was divided into hundreds.

☑ Each hundred was divided into tithings.

A tithing was (originally) 10 households; a hundred was (originally) 100 **hides** of land.

The administration of Anglo-Saxon England was based on the hide. Each hide of land (about 120 acres) carried obligations: for example, having five hides of land meant the obligation to provide one man for the fyrd.

Key terms

☑ **Shires** – an earldom was divided up into shires.

☑ **Hide** – an area of land covering about 120 acres.

☑ **Ceorls** – peasant farmers.

☑ **Fyrd** – the men of the Anglo-Saxon army and fleet.

☑ **Writ** – written orders from the king. A royal seal proved it was official.

Law and order in Anglo-Saxon England

Strengths		Weaknesses
Depended on everyone in the community knowing each other very well.	**Collective responsibility** – if one member of a tithing broke the law, the rest were responsible for bringing him to court or would be punished themselves.	Powerless to prevent powerful men (like earls) from breaking the law.
	Hue and cry – anyone in the community could call on all the others to help them track down a criminal. The sheriff could also call on the community in the same way.	
	Wergild – compensation paid to avoid blood feud.	

Trial by ordeal – God was asked to judge cases where community courts could not decide.

The king – treason was a very serious crime; the death penalty could be imposed.

Now try this

Describe **two** features of the shire reeve/sheriff's role that had an economic function.

The economy and social system

Anglo-Saxon England was one of Europe's wealthiest countries with strong trading links across the seas. England's towns were trading centres, though almost everyone worked in farming.

What gave England its strong economy?

- 👍 There was a good climate for farming, especially in the south and east for crops and in the west for livestock.
- 👍 England had strong trade links across the North Sea to Scandinavia and across the Channel to Normandy and Flanders.
- 👍 The efficient tax system boosted the earnings of the king and also the income of his nobles and the Church, who kept some of the tax.
- 👍 Central control of money supply and trading centres (burhs) meant that money was reliable (kept its value) and trade could be taxed, benefitting the nobility.

Anglo-Saxon society

Out of a population of 2 million in 1060, only 4000–6000 were nobles (thegns). 9.7% were slaves. The rest were peasant farmers (ceorls).

90% of population →

Thegns
Anglo-Saxon warrior/noble class with five hides of land or more.

Ceorls
Most depended on thegns for land and work. Some ceorls were freer.

Slaves
Treated as property: people who could be bought and sold.

Burhs

Burhs were the fortified main town of each shire.

People from the countryside would take refuge in the burh when Vikings were around.

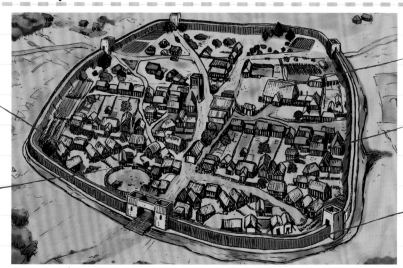

All significant trade had to be carried out in burhs by law. This trade was then taxed.

Around 10% of the population of England lived in towns in 1060. Everyone else lived in family groups in the countryside.

Strong walls and ramparts made the towns difficult to attack by Viking raiding parties.

The Church

Five key features of the Anglo-Saxon Church:

1. Bishops were rich and important. They controlled large Church districts. The Witan always included important bishops.

2. Very few people in Anglo-Saxon England were literate, so the Church provided all the king's clerks and record-keepers.

3. Most local priests farmed like peasants, were not well educated and were married.

4. This was true for monks and nuns too: they lived as part of the general community.

5. The Church was resistant to reforms from Europe. English bishops stuck to their old ways.

Social roles

Anglo-Saxon society was flexible. Peasant farmers could become thegns if they did well and acquired more than five hides of land. At the same time, peasants who did badly might have to sell themselves into slavery. Slaves could be freed by their masters and become peasants.

Thegns were the Anglo-Saxon warrior class. Their land holdings meant they could afford weapons, armour and a horse. They were expected to always be ready to serve their lord in battle, and fight to the death to protect him.

Now try this

Explain **three** reasons why thegns were an important part of Anglo-Saxon society.

The power of the Godwins

By the 1060s, the 'House of Godwin' had come to dominate Anglo-Saxon politics, building a powerbase from Wessex out to all the major earldoms of England, except one: Mercia.

Godwins in control

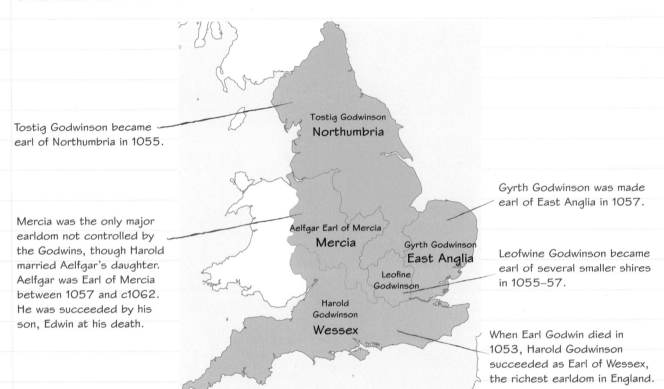

Tostig Godwinson became earl of Northumbria in 1055.

Tostig Godwinson
Northumbria

Gyrth Godwinson was made earl of East Anglia in 1057.

Mercia was the only major earldom not controlled by the Godwins, though Harold married Aelfgar's daughter. Aelfgar was Earl of Mercia between 1057 and c1062. He was succeeded by his son, Edwin at his death.

Aelfgar Earl of Mercia
Mercia

Gyrth Godwinson
East Anglia

Leofine Godwinson

Leofwine Godwinson became earl of several smaller shires in 1055–57.

Harold Godwinson
Wessex

When Earl Godwin died in 1053, Harold Godwinson succeeded as Earl of Wessex, the richest earldom in England.

Political marriages: three Ediths and a Judith

The House of Godwin increased its power and influence with important political marriages.

- ✓ Earl Godwin's daughter Edith married King Edward.
- ✓ Harold Godwinson had a political marriage to Edith of Mercia daughter of Aelfgar and then a second marriage to Edith the Fair, who was influential in East Anglia.
- ✓ Tostig Godwinson married Judith, daughter of Baldwin of Flanders.

Godwins in trouble?

In the 1050s, King Edward tried to free himself from Earl Godwin's dominance. Some historians think he turned to his friends in Normandy for help (Edward had been an exile in Normandy for most of his youth). This might have been where Edward promised William the throne of England.

Though the Godwins were exiled for a year, when they returned with a huge fleet, Edward pardoned Godwin rather than risk a civil war.

Now try this

'Earl Siward of Northumbria died in 1055. His eldest son had been killed in battle the year before, and his second son, Waltheof, was only five. Northumbria had major problems with lawlessness and England was under threat in the north from Scotland. Tostig Godwinson had made a very important political marriage with the daughter of Baldwin of Flanders (an important trading country in present-day Belgium).'

Use this information in an answer to the question: Why did King Edward agree to make Tostig Earl of Northumbria?

Edward the Confessor

The last years of Edward the Confessor saw a struggle between Harold and Tostig that undermined some of the power of the House of Godwin as Harold set his sights on becoming king after Edward.

Harold's embassy to Normandy

Here are three key features of Harold's **embassy** to Normandy in 1064 (or 1065).

1. King Edward sent Harold to Normandy but we do not know what message he wanted him to give to William of Normandy.
2. Harold was taken prisoner by Count Guy of Ponthieu but William rescued him. Harold fought for William and William rewarded him with gifts of weapons and armour.
3. Harold swore a very serious **oath** as part of the embassy but we do not know for certain what promise he was making.

Norman sources say: Harold swore allegiance to William in recognition that William was the future king of England.

English sources say: The embassy was to recover two hostages from Normandy and the oath was nothing to do with the succession.

Why was the embassy important?

1. It shows that Harold was King Edward's trusted right-hand man for politics as well as for leading military campaigns.
2. Normans claimed that the embassy was about the plan for William of Normandy to succeed to the throne of England after Edward died. William used it to legitimise becoming king after the Conquest.
3. Normans used the embassy to claim that Harold was an 'oath-breaker' when he took the crown himself rather than supporting William's claim. This had implications for Norman rule.

Key events in the rising against Earl Tostig

1. October 1065: Northumbrian thegns revolt against Tostig, marching on York.
2. Northumbrians invite Morcar (the brother of Edwin, earl of Mercia after 1062) to be earl instead.
3. King Edward orders his earls to put down the uprising, but they find ways not to obey.
4. Instead, Harold agrees to the rebels' demands on King Edward's behalf: Tostig is to be replaced by Earl Morcar.
5. By 1 November, Tostig is exiled. Harold has weakened the House of Godwin, but perhaps strengthened his own claim to the throne.

Reasons for the uprising: Tostig went too far in his crackdown on lawlessness, abusing his power to threaten nobles and assassinating rivals. He became friendly with Malcolm III of Scotland instead of fighting him, and he over-taxed the Northumbrians.

Why didn't Harold stand up for his brother? It is likely that Harold suspected that King Edward did not have long to live. Edward had no children and perhaps Harold saw his chances of being made king would be stronger without Tostig. Harold may also have known that he needed to show he could act for the good of England, rather than just for his family, if he was going to get the Witan's support for his becoming king.

Key terms

✓ **Embassy** – A diplomatic mission to meet with the ruler of another country.

✓ **Oath** – a solemn promise to do something.

Now try this

Explain why there was an uprising against Tostig in 1065.

The rival claimants for the throne

Harold Godwinson was crowned king on the same day as Edward the Confessor's funeral on 6 January 1066, but there were other strong claimants to the throne due to agreements Edward had made in the past and because Edward had died without a son: a succession crisis.

Harold Godwinson (c1022–66)

Claim	Appointed successor by the king on his deathbed.
Strength of claim	Good – supported by witnesses (ones already loyal to Harold).
Chance of success	Excellent – Harold had the support required (the Witan) in order to be made king.

Harold had been Edward's *sub regulus*, he was proven in battle, he had shown he was willing to go against Tostig for the good of the country, and he was King Edward's brother in law. England backed him.

Edgar Aethling (c1051–c1126)

Claim	Royal blood – A descendant of King Alfred the Great.
Strength of claim	Strong in theory but Edgar had nothing to back it up with.
Chance of success	Weak – Edgar was only a teenager. The threat of invasion was too great to risk him as king.

Although Edward the Confessor had planned to make Edgar his heir in the 1050s, he didn't take his plan further. The Witan could not risk England's defences to a boy king.

Harald Hardrada (c1015–66)

Claim	Based on a secret deal made between two other Vikings.
Strength of claim	Weak – what mattered though, was the force Hardrada could call on to back up his claim.
Chance of success	Good – Hardrada had 300 ships and 15 000 warriors, huge battle experience and expected the Danelaw regions to welcome him.

Hardrada could also make his claim as a descendant of King Cnut, the Danish king of England. Hardrada probably did not consider acting on his claim until Tostig persuaded him that the throne could easily be his.

William of Normandy (c1028–87)

Claim	An agreement with King Edward following Harold's embassy to Normandy.
Strength of claim	Backed by the pope, but lacking evidence.
Chance of success	Quite good because of William's military strength, but only if he was able to get his knights across the Channel to England.

William's claim was based on an agreement with Edward the Confessor in the 1050s when, William said, Edward promised him the throne in return for Normandy's help against Edward's rebellious earls. The pope's backing for William was linked to a plan to introduce reform to England's Church.

☐ weak chance   ☐ good chance

Harold's coronation and reign

- Harold was crowned the day after Edward the Confessor died: 6 January 1066.
- Most of the Witan were already gathered at Westminster, making it easier for Harold to gather the support he needed.

For more on the Witan see page 1.

King Harold's reign

- Soon after his coronation he went to York to make sure he had the north's support.
- He put together the largest army England had ever seen in the south of England. A fleet also patrolled the Channel.

Now try this

Identify **two** challenges that Harold II faced as he began his reign in January 1066.

Gate Fulford and Stamford Bridge

Harold's fyrd were ready to defend England's southern coast all through the spring and summer of 1066, but as September came, the fyrd had to be disbanded for the harvest. By mid-September, Hardrada and Tostig had launched their invasion, which Harold heard about on 19 September.

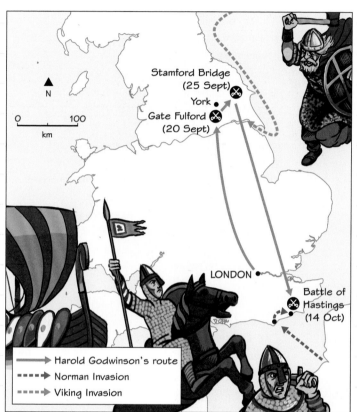

Reasons for the Battle of Gate Fulford

- Morcar, Earl of Northumbria, and his elder brother Edwin, Earl of Mercia, had gathered an army to defend the north.
- Hardrada and Tostig had landed with 10 000 warriors on the River Humber and then marched up towards York.
- Morcar and Edwin decided to meet them in open battle at Gate Fulford rather than defend the fortified city of York.

Events of the Battle of Gate Fulford

- Edwin and Morcar were outnumbered.
- As the English shield wall surged forward against Tostig's weaker troops, Hardrada hit the English troops with his best warriors from the side (a clever flanking tactic).
- Thousands of English troops were killed or wounded, making them unavailable to fight against the Norman invasion. Hardrada and Tostig took many English hostages.
- Harold was forced to come north to deal with Hardrada and Tostig, with consequences for the Battle of Hastings.

Although leaving the southern coast turned out to be a terrible decision for Harold II, there *were* good reasons at the time to think the threat of invasion from Normandy had passed for 1066. The Channel was notorious for winter storms, making a September crossing extremely risky. The wind was also still blowing from the north when Harold set off, thus keeping William bottled up in port in Normandy.

The English were positioned with marshland behind them, which meant that when they were pushed back they became stuck in mud and were massacred.

The Battle of Stamford Bridge

- Having led a rapid march to the north, gathering troops along the way, Harold's army surprised the Viking army at Stamford Bridge.
- Harold was victorious. Both Hardrada and Tostig were killed in the battle.
- The Vikings had left their armour with their ships. The English broke their shield wall.

Significance of the Battle of Stamford Bridge

- King Harold achieved a great victory, defending England from invasion.
- However, William invaded in the south while Harold was in the north.
- Harold had to rapidly move south again, tiring his housecarls.
- Harold's victory may have made him complacent about William's threat.
- The battles in the north may have prevented troops reaching Hastings from Mercia and Northumbria.

Now try this

Identify **three** reasons why Harold was victorious at Stamford Bridge.

The Battle of Hastings

You need to know about key features of the Battle of Hastings, including the composition of the two armies (the types of troops that made up each army).

Timeline

1066

28 Sep the Normans land at Pevensey

6 Oct Harold reaches London

14 Oct the Battle of Hastings

27 Sep William's fleet sets sail

2 Oct Harold leaves York

12 Oct Harold leaves London

Key events of the Battle of Hastings

1 William's scouts spotted Harold's advancing army – Harold failed to achieve a surprise attack.

2 Harold's army was able to position itself along a ridge at the top of a hill. That meant that William had to attack up hill.

3 The battle lasted eight hours – a very long time for a medieval battle. This was perhaps because the two sides were quite evenly matched. There were different phases to the battle.

4 William's archers were first to attack, but the archers had to stay out of English javelin range and the English shield wall knew how to catch the arrows on their shields.

5 William's foot soldiers and knights were beaten back by the shield wall initially. The English **housecarls** did great damage to horses and men with their two-handed axes.

6 At one point the Norman army was panicking that William had been killed. William tipped back his helmet to show he was still alive.

7 A feigned retreat (or a real retreat) meant English fyrdsmen left the shield wall to chase after retreating Normans. The English were then surrounded and cut down.

8 The shield wall was gradually thinned out. Norman knights then charged through it and caused great damage. Norman archers also became more effective as the shield wall failed.

9 Harold and his brothers, Gyrth and Leofwine, and their housecarls, made final stands at the top of the hill, fighting to the death. Harold and his brothers died.

10 The rest of the English army then ran for it. The *Bayeux Tapestry* ends with the words (in Latin): 'and the English turned and fled'.

Norman knights v. English housecarls

Norman knights
Advantages – highly trained, heavily-armoured mounted knights could launch devastating charges using their height advantage to beat down foes.

Disadvantages – horses were vulnerable to attack, advantages of a cavalry charge were lost if horses had to run uphill.

English housecarls
Advantages – a disciplined shield wall was very hard to break. Housecarls knew how to fight together and their axes were highly effective.

Disadvantages – once the shield wall began to break, housecarls were vulnerable to cavalry and archer attacks.

Key terms

 Housecarls – trained soldiers who were also bodyguards to their lord.

Norman foot soldiers v. English fyrds

William's foot soldiers were a mixture of Normans and mercenaries from across Europe. There were lightly armoured archers and crossbowmen and heavily armoured foot soldiers. Foot soldiers may not have trained with knights, making coordinated attacks difficult.

While thegns had good weapons, many of Harold's general fyrd would have had farm tools and long knives. There were few archers. General fyrdsmen were not well trained.

Now try this

Describe **one** advantage and **one** disadvantage of the Norman foot soldiers and **one** advantage and **one** disadvantage of the English fyrd troops.

William's victory

You need to know about the range of causes of Harold's eventual defeat, including William's superior leadership skills, the strength and skills of the two armies, and Harold's mistakes.

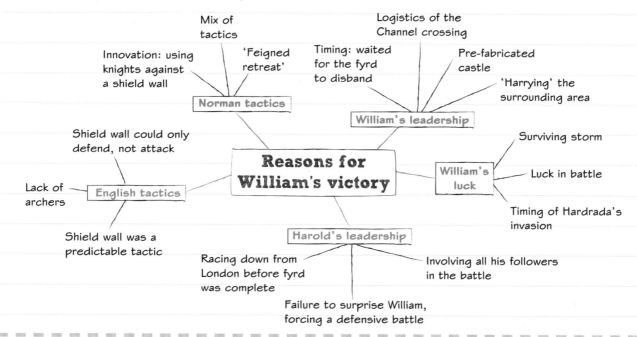

Battle advantages

Harold	William of Normandy
👍 Harold was fighting on home ground: Wessex.	👍 William's troops were trained in tactics that the English had never experienced before, including the feigned retreat.
👍 The housecarls were experienced, disciplined and skilled warriors.	👍 His troops had to fight to survive: they would not be able to retreat or escape.
👍 The English had the best position on the battlefield: on a ridge at the top of the hill.	👍 William had obtained the pope's blessing for his invasion and he and his men believed that God was on their side.

Battle disadvantages

Harold	William of Normandy
👎 The men of the general fyrd were inexperienced and lacked discipline.	👎 Having to fight up hill made knights and archers less effective.
👎 The core of his army was tired from fighting at Stamford Bridge and marching south. They may also have been demoralised by having to fight yet another battle.	👎 Although his knights had trained for years in their battle tactics, many of his foot soldiers were mercenaries who had not trained to fight in combination with knights.
👎 A lack of archers – it is possible that English archers were among the fyrd troops who arrived in London after Harold had already rushed off down to Hastings.	👎 Knights had trained to charge against other knights: charging a shield wall was probably something entirely new.

Now try this

Explain the importance of the 'feigned retreat' as an explanation for William's victory at the Battle of Hastings.

9

Establishing control

You need to be able to explain why the earls submitted to William following his march on London, how William rewarded his followers and how he protected the borders of his new kingdom.

The march on London

- Following the Battle of Hastings, William and his men marched to Dover where they became very ill with dysentery.
- In London the remaining English nobility chose Edgar Aethling as Harold's successor, but they did not attack William at Dover.
- Having recovered, William led his army on a brutal march through south-east England, destroying homes and farms.
- Towns and villages were intimidated and surrendered. William led his army round London to Berkhamsted rather than attacking London directly.

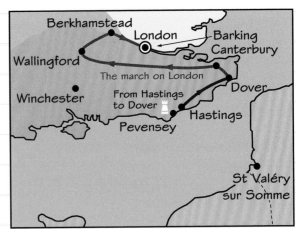

The submission of the earls

Why did Edgar Aethling, Edwin, Morcar and the other English nobles submit without a fight?

- 👎 William had seized the royal treasury so Edgar Aethling had little to offer followers in the way of reward.
- 👎 William's march round London may have threatened to cut the city off from supplies.
- 👎 England's best warriors died at the Battle of Hastings.
- 👎 Did the surviving English nobles believe William's victory was God's will?
- 👎 The English should have attacked William at Dover. Perhaps Edgar and the earls couldn't agree about what action to take.

William rewards Anglo-Saxons

Rewarding loyalty	Although...
Edwin and Morcar keep their earldoms.	Edwin and Morcar's earldoms are smaller than before.
Edwin promised William's daughter in marriage.	This marriage never actually occurs.
Gospatric made earl of northern Northumbria.	Gospatric had to pay William a lot of money for the earldom.
Everyone who fought against William loses their land.	All this land goes to William and his followers, not to Anglo-Saxons.

Rewarding followers

William had promised his followers great riches in return for their support for the invasion.

- ✓ He sent lavish gifts to the pope (probably from the English royal treasury).
- ✓ He set a heavy geld tax, to pay his mercenaries (professional soldiers).
- ✓ He declared that all land in England belonged to him. He then granted land and earldoms to his followers.

Hugh d'Avranches, William FitzOsbern and Roger de Montgomery were followers of William and had supported him in the invasion. They became the first three Marcher earls.

Controlling the borderlands

William created three new earldoms (Hereford, Shrewsbury and Chester) to protect the Marches – the border with Wales. The Marcher earl had special rights and privileges. They:

- ✓ could create new towns to promote Norman colonisation of the Marches
- ✓ had total control: their sheriffs reported to them rather than to the king
- ✓ did not have to pay tax on their lands, so they could invest in defence
- ✓ could build castles as they wished.

Now try this

Who were the first three Marcher earls? Explain what powers they had.

Castles

The Normans' motte and bailey castles were almost unknown in Anglo-Saxon England. They had a huge military and psychological impact that made it easier for the Normans to establish control and secure their conquest.

A palisade (strong fence) was made of solid timbers driven deep into the ground: it was strong and quick to build. Sometimes a double fence with earth packed in between was built.

Access to the keep was either up steep steps cut into the motte or, in some castles, up a sort of bridge.

A strong wooden tower called the keep provided a lookout point, an elevated attack position for archers to defend the whole area of the castle and a final point of defence from attack.

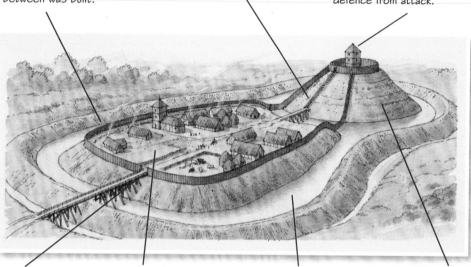

Access into the castle was controlled through the gatehouse. Sometimes a drawbridge over the ditch could be pulled up to defend the gatehouse from attack.

The bailey was the enclosure below the motte and also protected by the palisade and outer defences, where the stables and barracks would be for the garrison of troops. During attacks, local people and livestock could take shelter here.

A ditch was cut that surrounded both the bailey and the motte. Sometimes the ditch was filled with water, protecting the palisade.

The motte was a large mound of earth, typically 5–7 metres high. Because it was earth, it was fireproof. With enough peasant labour a motte was quick to build. Historians think most motte and bailey castles took between four and nine months to construct.

Why were castles important?

- They were located in strategically important places, for example, at river crossings. This made it easier to keep the local population (and any rebel activity) under surveillance.
- They were used as the base for attacks. A garrison of troops in the castle could ride out to suppress trouble, and if they came under attack they could return to the castle's defences.
- The Normans built castles to control areas. When a town was overlooked by a Norman castle, it had a psychological impact on the locals: making them feel dominated.

How were castles different from burhs?

- Burhs protected Anglo-Saxons; castles were built to control Anglo-Saxons.
- Burhs were large and designed to defend whole communities; castles were small and mainly private.
- Castles were part of the Norman domination of areas. Burhs took longer to construct, and were designed to defend inhabitants from attack by foreign invaders.

The Anglo-Saxon Chronicle describes the Normans building castles everywhere, oppressing the unhappy local people and making things 'always go from bad to worse'.

Now try this

Using the diagram above, describe **two** features of the castle that made it difficult to attack.

Anglo-Saxon resistance, 1068

William initially aimed to include the Anglo-Saxon earls in governing England. However, in 1068, earls Edwin and Morcar fled William's court and led a revolt against him. Other important Anglo-Saxon nobles joined the revolt, including earls Waltheof and Gospatric and Edgar Aethling.

Causes of the revolt

Edwin's resentment
Edwin was unhappy because William promised Edwin he could marry his daughter but William went back on his word and also reduced the size of Edwin's earldom.

Bad government
It was reported that Odo of Bayeux and William FitzOsbern had seized land unlawfully and allowed soldiers to rape Anglo-Saxon women without punishment.

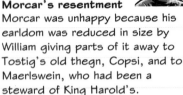

Morcar's resentment
Morcar was unhappy because his earldom was reduced in size by William giving parts of it away to Tostig's old thegn, Copsi, and to Maerlswein, who had been a steward of King Harold's.

The loss of lands
The Anglo-Saxon Chronicle for 1067 reports: 'When William returned (from Normandy) he gave away every man's land'. Odo and FitzOsbern's land grabs were repeated all over the country, with William's followers seeking to expand their grants by every means possible.

Causes of the revolt

Castles
Castles were resented as being a symbol of Norman domination. Housing was cleared to build castles and people were forced to provide resources for the castle garrison.

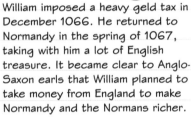

Taxes
William imposed a heavy geld tax in December 1066. He returned to Normandy in the spring of 1067, taking with him a lot of English treasure. It became clear to Anglo-Saxon earls that William planned to take money from England to make Normandy and the Normans richer.

William's response and its outcome

- William took his forces north into Mercia, Edwin's earldom, and Northumbria, which Morcar governed parts of (as did Gospatric and Waltheof).
- William first took control of the burhs of Warwick and then Nottingham and built castles in both places, destroying houses to make room for their construction.
- As soon as William took control of Warwick, Edwin and Morcar came down to Warwick with their men and submitted to William.
- Edwin and Morcar's actions meant the rest of the revolt collapsed. Edgar Aethling and other rebels escaped to Scotland and the protection and support of King Malcolm III.
- William pardoned Edwin and Morcar, and they returned to being William's 'guests' at his court, until 1071 when they escaped again.

Consequences of the revolt

- William decided that he needed to put a Norman in charge of the north. The man he chose, Robert Cumin, was a trigger for the next rebellion in the north. See page 13
- Edgar Aethling's escape to Scotland created a new centre of resistance to Norman control at Malcolm III's court. Edgar would attack northern England again.
- Castles proved very effective at bringing areas under control. Edwin and Morcar's rapid surrender to William probably came after they concluded that the Normans were too strong to resist.
- There were other revolts at the same time as Edwin and Morcar's revolt: for example, Eadric the Wild's rebellion against the Marcher earldoms, and in Exeter. Some Anglo-Saxons fought against these revolts, meaning that William was able to rely on some Anglo-Saxon troops to suppress Anglo-Saxon resistance.

Now try this

Explain why Odo of Bayeux and William FitzOsbern helped cause the revolt of 1068.

Anglo-Saxon resistance, 1069–71

The most serious Anglo-Saxon resistance came from the two rebellions associated with Edgar Aethling in the north in 1069. The last Anglo-Saxon rebellion against William's rule occurred in Ely in 1070–71, and is associated with Hereward the Wake.

Uprising in York

January 1069	February 1069
• Robert Cumin is appointed as the new earl of northern Northumbria. • Looting by his men triggers a rebellion in Durham: Cumin and his men are killed.	• An uprising in York, the governor and Norman troops are killed. • Edgar Aethling comes down from Scotland to join the rebellion. • Norman sheriff and his garrison are attacked.

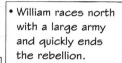

- William races north with a large army and quickly ends the rebellion.
- William lays waste to the whole city of York and builds new castles.
- William returns south for Easter.

 William was able to defeat the rebels in the north easily.

 William entrusted York to William FitzOsbern while he went back to Winchester for Easter, to celebrate the festival as England's king.

Anglo-Danish attack on York

September 1069
• King Sweyn of Denmark sends a large invasion fleet to England. • The Danish invasion force meets up with Edgar Aethling. • 21 September: the Anglo-Danish attack on York. 3000 Normans are killed. • The Danes retreat to the Lincolnshire coast.

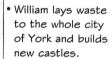

- Anglo-Saxons in the north begin guerilla warfare, sheltered by locals.
- New rebellions begin in Devon, Shrewsbury and Chester.
- As soon as William's forces subdue unrest in one region, it starts again somewhere else.
- The Danes bide their time, protected by marshland.

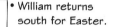

William's solutions

(1) Pay the Danes to leave England.

and

(2) The Harrying of the North.

Hereward the Wake and rebellion at Ely

- Hereward had returned to Ely around 1069 from exile. He started a rebellion because he had lost his lands to a new Norman lord.
- In 1070 the Danes returned and set up base in Ely. The Danes and Hereward joined forces for a raid on Peterborough Abbey.
- Hereward had hoped to save the treasures of the monastery from the Normans, but the Danes took all the treasure and sailed back to Denmark with it.
- Morcar and his men came to Ely and joined Hereward. They defended Ely but the Normans eventually defeated them.
- Morcar was captured while Hereward escaped – but he was not heard of again.

Anglo-Saxon resistance – a summary

Anglo-Saxon nobles who submitted to William were allowed to keep their positions as William wanted to rule with consent rather than by force.

William deprived the Anglo-Saxon nobles of any power and reduced their lands. This caused the rebellions.

William underestimated the independence of the north, but the real threat came with the Danish invasion.

As a result of the resistance, William decided that England could not be ruled with consent. The Anglo-Saxon aristocracy needed to be removed from power to prevent further resistance in the future.

Now try this

One outcome of the Anglo-Saxon resistance 1068–71 was that William decided to replace the remaining Anglo-Saxon aristocracy with Normans. Describe **one** other outcome.

The Harrying of the North

The brutality of the Harrying of the North shows that William was prepared to take the most extreme measures to keep England under his control. His decision to lay waste to the north had both immediate consequences (1069–70) and a longer-term legacy (1069–87).

Reasons

- To destroy the spirit of rebellion in the north.
- Revenge for the death of Robert Cumin and hundreds of other Normans.
- To prevent Vikings using Yorkshire as a base for future attacks.
- As a warning to other areas of England of what could happen to them.
- A military response to guerrilla warfare, which depended on support for rebels from local people.

Features

- Livestock killed.
- Homes destroyed so people had nowhere to shelter.
- Took place in the winter of 1069–70.
- Area of Harrying stretched from the Humber River to the Tees River. Also in Staffordshire and parts of Shropshire.
- Seed destroyed so there was nothing to plant for food the next year.

Harrying of the North

Immediate consequences

- Death of thousands from starvation: perhaps as many as 100 000 people died.
- Flood of refugees from the north to other parts of England, e.g. the west.
- Reports of families selling themselves into slavery to survive.
- Reports of cannibalism by desperate, starving people.

Long term consequences

- Criticism of William's brutality and William's own sense of his sin and need for penance.
- No further rebellion from the north; after 1071 no further Anglo-Saxon rebellions.
- Danish invaders in 1070 went to Ely as there was now no base for them in Yorkshire.
- A turning point: after 1070 William decided to replace the English aristocracy with Normans.
- 20 years later, Yorkshire had still not recovered; 60 per cent was listed as 'waste' in the Domesday Book and there were between 80 000 and 150 000 fewer people than in 1066.

The early medieval period was a violent time, but William's Harrying of the North was seen as especially brutal, even by his contemporaries. William was criticised by the pope for his actions, and was said to have repented for the deaths of so many people for the rest of his life.

Now try this

Look back at page 13 to answer this.

King Sweyn's invasion in 1070–71 went to Ely rather than to the north. Explain why this shows that the Harrying of the North achieved one of its goals.

Landownership, 1066–87

One of the legacies (long term consequences) of Anglo-Saxon resistance was the way the Anglo-Saxon aristocracy was removed from power and replaced by Normans. This mainly happened through changes in landownership.

Landownership changes by 1087

- ✓ Over half the land in England in 1087 was held by just 190 of the tenants-in-chief. Only two of these were Anglo-Saxons.
- ✓ Only around 5% of land was still held by Anglo-Saxon aristocrats in 1087, most of it in small estates.
- ✓ The king's own royal estates made up 20% of the land and the Church owned 25%.

Ways land could be lost or gained

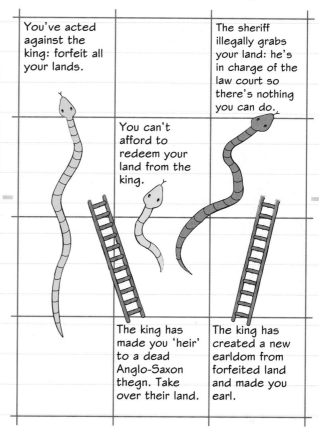

You've acted against the king: forfeit all your lands.

You can't afford to redeem your land from the king.

The sheriff illegally grabs your land: he's in charge of the law court so there's nothing you can do.

The king has made you 'heir' to a dead Anglo-Saxon thegn. Take over their land.

The king has created a new earldom from forfeited land and made you earl.

More power to the king

- Changes in landownership made William more powerful and rebellion less likely.
- Anglo-Saxons had to pay William to redeem land (get back land they owned before) and heirs paid the king to inherit land.
- When landholders died without an heir, the land went back to the king, and those who acted against the king could forfeit land (have their land taken from them).

Impact on thegns	Impact on peasants
With Normans becoming the major landholders, English thegns became their tenants. The Normans had followers of their own whom they needed to reward with land. • When thegns died, Norman followers would 'inherit' their land, not the thegns' children. • Thegns who did not obey their Norman lords could forfeit their land. Many thegns left England to work as mercenaries in Europe. Those that stayed were forced to obey their new lords.	Life for many peasants probably went on much as it did before the Conquest, since one lord was much like another from the peasants' point of view. However, it is likely that Normans were stricter about their peasants meeting all the obligations due from the land they worked. Ceorls – the 'free' peasants who could decide to leave one lord and go and rent land from another – became rarer and rarer. Norman lords worked to reduce the independence of ceorls.

Now try this

Edwin forfeited his lands in 1071 after he died (he was killed by his own men). Morcar forfeited his lands in 1070 after joining which rebellion?

Maintaining royal power

William used force to get control of his new kingdom, but he wanted to rule as England's legitimate king as well as its conqueror. He adopted the powers and symbols of Edward the Confessor and promoted the claim that he was the rightful successor to King Edward.

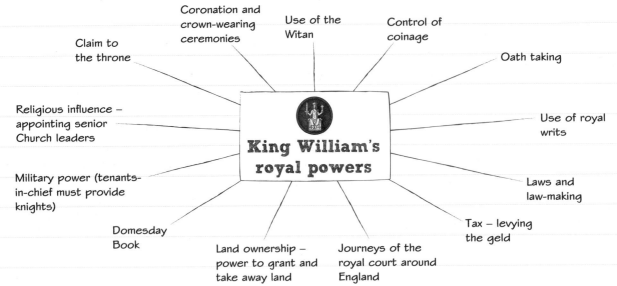

Coronation and crown-wearing ceremonies

Use of the Witan

Control of coinage

Claim to the throne

Oath taking

Religious influence – appointing senior Church leaders

King William's royal powers

Use of royal writs

Military power (tenants-in-chief must provide knights)

Laws and law-making

Domesday Book

Tax – levying the geld

Land ownership – power to grant and take away land

Journeys of the royal court around England

Royal factors

♛ Claim to the throne: Norman propaganda stressed that William had been Edward's rightful successor, as well as his relative.

♛ Royal ceremonies: William began a new ceremony of being seen wearing his crown three times a year, at events where he also consulted with his Witan.

♛ Coinage: William's coins featured his image, reinforcing his role as king.

♛ Writs: William's image also appeared on the royal seal of his writs. William used writs to issue his orders across the land. The Anglo-Saxon writ system was designed to maintain royal power across England and William used writs enthusiastically.

♛ Oath taking: William held oath-taking ceremonies in which landholders swore their allegiance to William as their king.

♛ Journeys around England: by travelling to different parts of his kingdom, William could show himself as king to his subjects. He could also show favour to important subjects by visiting them and holding talks.

Other factors

† William's military strength: Anglo-Saxons respected great warrior-kings. However, such kings would ideally also show wisdom in their law-making and mercy in their treatment of their subjects, for example, Edward the Confessor was respected for living on the revenues of his own estates rather than benefitting from frequent geld taxes.

✝ Religious influence: William had control over appointments to senior positions in the Church. His reforms (with Archbishop Lanfranc) of the Church in England increased Norman control of the messages given out in churches, which were used to praise William as king.

🐄 Landownership: William was able to use forfeited Anglo-Saxon lands to reward his followers. This helped ensure their support for William's rule as England's king. Challenges to William's rule came from those who thought they had not been given enough land.

Now try this

Explain the consequences of William's claim to the throne for landownership in England.

The Revolt of the Earls

In 1075, three of William's own earls tried, unsuccessfully, to remove him from power. This was the last revolt William would face in England before his death a decade later. This page looks at the reasons for revolt; the next page is on its features, its defeat and effects.

The rebel earls and their motives

Roger de Breteuil, Earl of Hereford, was the son of William FitzOsbern. Roger resented the way William had reduced the size of his Hereford earldom after FitzOsbern died. FitzOsbern had been one of William's most trusted followers.

Ralph de Gael, Earl of East Anglia, had grown up in Brittany and became Earl of East Anglia after his father died around 1069. It is likely his involvement in the revolt was for similar reasons to Roger de Breteuil. He married Roger's sister in 1075.

Waltheof, had taken part in the rebellions in the north in 1069, but had submitted to William, was pardoned and made Earl of Northumbria (his father had been Siward, Earl of Northumbria). He was the last surviving Anglo-Saxon earl. Presumably, Northumbrians would have supported their earl if there was a good chance of success against the Normans.

Loss of privileges
One of the features of the Marcher earldoms, which included Hereford, was that sheriffs answered to the earl, not to the king. William changed this so that he had more influence in all his earldoms. Roger resented this loss of privilege and there may have been others, too.

Loss of land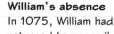
William was concerned that earls should not have too much power. This was why he took the opportunity of their fathers' deaths to reduce the size of Ralph and Roger's land.

William's absence
In 1075, William had returned temporarily to Normandy, leaving the government of England to his regent, Archbishop Lanfranc. The rebels saw his absence as an opportunity to strike.

Reasons for the revolt

Loss of power
Under Anglo-Saxon rule, earls had been very powerful. The three earls planned to recreate this situation by dividing William's kingdom between the three of them.

Anglo-Saxon rebelliousness
The Revolt of the Earls took place soon after the rebellions of 1068–71. The three earls must have assumed Anglo-Saxons would join their revolt, especially with Waltheof involved.

Powerful allies
Ralph contacted King Sweyn of Denmark for support in the revolt. It is likely that Waltheof was important in making this deal with the Danes. King Sweyn's son Cnut put together a large fleet. The rebels also had support from William's enemies in Brittany and France.

Now try this

Explain **one** reason why William wanted to reduce the power of his own earls.

Features and effects of the Revolt

Unfortunately for Earls Roger, Ralph and Waltheof, their revolt did not succeed and was quickly defeated. Key to their defeat was the way Anglo-Saxons joined Normans to prevent the revolt.

Features of the revolt

Waltheof informed Archbishop Lanfranc about the revolt.

⬇

Key feature 1: Waltheof decided against being involved in the revolt, perhaps hoping to be rewarded for his loyalty in informing. However, William ordered him to be executed instead.

Lanfranc tried to convince Roger not to act against William.

⬇

Key feature 2: Lanfranc had time to prepare for the revolt. His arguments to Roger were that Roger should remember his father's loyalty.

When Roger did not give up his plans, Lanfranc excommunicated him.

⬇

Bishop Wulfstan and the abbot of Evesham blocked Roger from taking his troops across the Severn River.

⬇

Key feature 3: Although all Anglo-Saxons might have been expected to join the revolt against William, most did not. Even more significantly, Anglo-Saxons in the Midlands joined with Norman garrisons in preventing the revolts from spreading out of Herefordshire and out of East Anglia.

Anglo-Saxons also joined Normans in the east to prevent Ralph's troops breaking out of East Anglia.

⬇

Key feature 4: The Danes had an impressive invasion force but they did not want to engage with the Normans in battle, at least not until Norman forces had already been significantly weakened by Anglo-Saxon uprisings.

When the Danes arrived with 200 ships the revolt had ground to a halt. The Danes did not invade but raided and returned to Denmark.

The defeat of the revolt

William returned to England before the Danes arrived, and oversaw the defeat of the revolt.

- Roger was captured and imprisoned for life.

- Ralph escaped to Brittany, though William captured some of his Breton followers and punished them by blinding them.

- Waltheof fled abroad, but William tricked him into coming back to England. When Waltheof returned he was imprisoned and then executed.

Challenges to William and his sons were now from William's own earls and barons.

The planned Danish invasion of 1075 was the end of the Viking threat to England.

Significance of the revolt

Anglo-Saxons defended William's rule from revolt, suggesting some English support for William.

Despite Anglo-Saxon support in defeating the revolt, William continued to suppress Anglo-Saxon nobles.

Now try this

Lanfranc excommunicated Earl Roger. Which **one** of the following is the best definition of excommunication?

a) Making someone an outlaw, which meant they could then be legally killed.

b) Cutting someone off from the Church community, so they could not confess their sins.

c) Sentencing someone to pay a fine to the Church in order to be forgiven.

The feudal hierarchy

When William became king, he established himself as the owner of all England's land. His key allies became his **tenants-in-chief**, who received huge grants of land direct from the king in return for their military service. They then granted land out to their followers in turn, creating a feudal **hierarchy** with the king at the top, with huge power to command and control the system.

Key terms

Barony – lands held by a baron (a major land owner, often a tenant-in-chief).

Fief or feud – land held by a **vassal** in return for service to a lord ('feud' is where feudalism comes from).

Homage – a public display of allegiance (loyalty) to a lord.

Tenant-in-chief – someone who held their fiefs directly from the king.

Vassal – someone who held land from someone else in the feudal system.

Hierarchy – where society is organised into levels of importance with each level obeying the level above them.

Knight service

Knight service was the duty to provide a knight or knights for the king for up to 40 days a year.

Some knights had not much more land to farm than peasants.

Some knight service involved guarding the king's castles.

Other knights were very powerful Norman nobles.

The knights had to be equipped and given money to live on during knight service.

Tenants-in-chief

```
                    Tenants-in-chief
         ┌──────────┬──────┴──────┬──────────┐
```

Military: fought for the king and led their knights.

Social: law courts to deal with **barony** land disputes.

Economic: paid the king tax from their large revenues.

Political: often served on the royal council as advisors.

The feudal hierarchy

Granted land and tax concessions
Provided peace, law and protection in return for loyalty and service

William I 👑

Knight service according to set quota
Tax (and reliefs)
Justice (baronial courts)

Tenants-in-chief
(Lords, bishops and abbots)

Military service in return for land
Tax (and reliefs)
Justice (manorial courts)

Granted land and other privileges

Under-tenants
(Vassals)

Provided land to be worked

Land service (farming on vassal's land) / Rent

Peasants
(Some free men, but the majority were bound to one lord)

Now try this

Describe **two** features of the feudal hierarchy that increased William's military strength.

The nature of feudalism

The feudal system probably took several decades to develop as it was something new to both Normans and English. William took the opportunity of the Conquest to clear away the complex relationships between England's landholders and redevelop them to consolidate his power.

Feudalism and military power

The feudal system was a way of ensuring that the king had military power without having to pay for it.

Knights were extremely expensive to equip, train and maintain, but William needed lots of them. The feudal system developed so William received knight service in return for grants of land – both knights to fight in battle and knights to garrison his castles.

The fyrd still continued to operate alongside knight service: probably more of a **militia** provided by the general fyrd. William's son, William Rufus, used English fyrd troops to defeat a rebellion against him after William the Conqueror's death.

Feudalism and political power

Feudalism gave the king political power: he could control his barons through grants of land, reliefs and forfeiture.

William needed to be able to control his barons, or they would get too powerful and demand political power for themselves. **Forfeiture** meant that William had the power to punish severely anyone who acted against him by taking away their lands and granting them as a reward for loyalty to someone else.

In both Normandy and in Anglo-Saxon England, noble sons usually inherited their fathers' landholdings automatically. William toughened up the procedures and made inheritance dependent on a formal ceremony of **homage** to the king, and on paying as much for their relief as the king thought was suitable.

Feudalism and the peasants

Feudalism was a social system that made sure the nobility stayed rich and in control.

Just as the vassal provided military service for his **fief**, peasants provided labour service for their lord in return for land and protection from attack, but this came at a cost. Instead of ceorls being able to decide to leave a lord and go and work for another one, peasants were now bound to their lord, unable to leave his or her service.

How 'feudal' was Anglo-Saxon England? It seems likely that most peasants in Anglo-Saxon England were already bound to their lords through obligations and relationships that were very similar to labour service. These were obligations that came with each hide of land and the Domesday Book suggests these obligations continued after the Conquest.

Vassals swearing allegiance to a medieval king in an act of homage.

Now try this

Explain what was involved in forfeiture.

The Church in England

The Church had a huge influence on society in the early Medieval period, and by 1088 William had ensured that Normans had replaced Anglo-Saxons in almost all the leading roles of the Church. This included Archbishop of Canterbury Stigand being replaced by the reformer, Lanfranc.

The Church helped control society by praising the king and teaching the people about their role in society.

Importance of the Church

The Church taught reading and writing and government depended on Church officials. Church clerks issued the king's writs.

The Church was a major landholder. Church tenants worked for the Church. The Church paid taxes to the king.

In society

In government

Because the Church kept collections of laws, the Church was able to advise on legal matters.

Church leaders were involved in shire courts and other legal processes where God's will needed to be interpreted.

Bishops and abbots were good advisors for the king because they were educated and literate.

Criticisms of Stigand

Stigand was accused of encouraging corruption in the Church.

- 👎 Stigand was a **pluralist** – he was bishop for more than one area, increasing his land and revenue.
- 👎 He was also accused of **simony**, giving out jobs in the Church in return for money.

His appointment also caused other problems.

- 👎 Lanfranc believed only the Church or the king should appoint bishops, but Stigand got his job because of the Godwins.
- 👎 Stigand had no real control over other archbishops and bishops in England – there was a lack of discipline.

Lanfranc's reforms: control of the Church

Lanfranc wanted a strict hierarchy in the Church, with the archbishop of Canterbury at the top, answering only to the king and the pope in Rome.

- Lanfranc convinced the king to put the Archbishop of Canterbury in charge of the whole Church in England.
- As head of the Church, Lanfranc then reorganised Church councils, held them more frequently and used them to push through his reforms.
- Archdeacons were brought in to control parish priests.

Normanisation of the Church

- After Stigand had been removed from his role as Archbishop in 1070, only one Anglo-Saxon bishop, Wulfstan, remained in place.
- Every church and cathedral in England was rebuilt in Norman style.
- Lanfranc's reforms put the whole Church under central control.
- The king appointed new bishops, his approval was needed for key Church decisions and Church leaders could forfeit lands if they disobeyed him.
- The king controlled communication between the English Church and the pope.

Lanfranc's reforms: a spiritual Church

Lanfranc wanted the Church to be separate from ordinary society so its members could live a spiritual life of prayer and service to God.

- Priests should be celibate and marriage for priests was banned because priests should live special lives devoted to God.
- Clergy were not to be tried by the 'ordinary' courts. Special, Church-only bishops' courts tried cases involving clergy.
- The number of monasteries and nunneries was increased and monks and nuns no longer mixed so much with ordinary people.

Now try this

Explain why King William wanted to control the communication between his bishops and the pope. How was this connected to William's obsession with control in England?

The extent of change

1066 was certainly an important turning point for England, but how much change was there to England's society and economy? Was England completely transformed, or was there also continuity as well as change? And was any of the change positive for Anglo-Saxons?

Comparing Anglo-Saxon and Norman societies

Anglo-Saxon society		Norman society	
	Slaves made up just less than 10% of the population.		The Normans thought slavery was wrong and freed some slaves.
	Peasants (ceorls) made up around 90% of the population. Some were free.		Feudalism bound peasants to their lords. Norman lords may have worked peasants harder. But not a huge change.
	4–6 thousand thegns; local landowners with more than 5 hides of land. Military service.		Thegns wiped out as a landowning class and replaced by knights and other Norman vassals of tenants-in-chief.
	Some earls were so powerful and wealthy that they posed a threat to the king.		Earls replaced by Normans, and earldoms made much smaller. Earls were tenants-in-chief, dependent on the king.

Continuity

- Economic **Farming life** went on as before, although Normans landlords may have been stricter in demanding the obligations due from each hide.

- **Government:** although William replaced Anglo-Saxons with Normans, the processes of government, such as writs, continued as before because they were superior to Norman government processes.

- Economic **Geld tax:** this was a major source of revenue for the king and allowed William to extract money from his new kingdom. Although Edward the Confessor had not over-used the geld tax, previous Danish and Anglo-Saxon kings had levied heavy geld taxes and William definitely continued in this tradition.

- **Towns:** William agreed that towns could keep their trading rights and privileges.

Change

- Economic **Trade** with Scandinavia was reduced (impacting the north of England) and trade with Normandy increased (boosting the south of England).

- **Military:** castles dominated the skyline of many English towns and strategic locations. Houses were cleared in burhs to make way for castles.

- **Religion:** Lanfranc's reforms dragged the English Church into the 11th century and every church and cathedral was rebuilt.

- **Social control:** William's imposition of a feudal hierarchy made the king much more powerful and everyone else more dependent on the favour of their lord.

- **Political:** Anglo-Saxons were removed from almost all positions of influence. Those that remained, like Bishop Wulfstan, only did so because they had proved exceptionally loyal to William.

Now try this

Which of the social or economic changes brought about by the Norman Conquest is most likely to be described as 'not negative' for Anglo-Saxons?

Changes to government

William centralised the existing Anglo-Saxon institutions of government to increase his control over England. This gave him and his successors much more power as king than Edward the Confessor had been able to access, and more power than William had as Duke of Normandy.

How power was centralised in Norman England

Crown lands
William kept far more land than King Edward in the form of royal demesne and forest (for hunting).

The Church
It was easier to control the Church because the king owned all Church land and power was centralised through Lanfranc's reforms.

Knights in service
All troops owed their loyalty to the king.

William I

Feudal system
Everyone who worked on the land depended ultimately on the king.

Economy
The king gained revenue through the geld tax and through reliefs, which helped ensure loyalty from his tenants-in-chief.

The Domesday Book
This provided a guide to what the king's tenants-in-chief were worth and what the king could expect to earn from them.

The role of earls

William's control of Normandy had been challenged many times by rivals, so he understood the dangers of letting even his most loyal followers get too powerful. This is why he reduced the power of England's earls by:

- making earldoms smaller – reduced land meant reduced power
- reducing the number of earldoms, e.g. Wessex and Mercia
- increasing the power of sheriffs, who answered directly to the king
- using knight service to make sure he had a large army as king, but no one else did
- using his powers over tenants-in-chief to make sure his earls were dependent on him for keeping their lands and to be able to pass them on to their heirs.

The Revolt of the Earls (1075) shows that William's reduction of earls' power was resented by some of England's earls.

The role of regents

Because William was both king of England and duke of Normandy he had to rely on regents to run Normandy when he was in England, and England when he was in Normandy. He spent up to three-quarters of his time away from England in the last ten years of his life.

1 Odo of Bayeux and William FitzOsbern seem to have done a terrible job as the first regents in 1067, undoing all of William's diplomatic approach towards the Anglo-Saxon nobility and helping to provoke Anglo-Saxon resistance.

2 Lanfranc was much more reliable as a regent: in 1075 he managed to contain the Revolt of the Earls until William could return from Normandy. The fact that the rebel earls had timed their revolt for a period when William was away shows how important King William was personally to the central control of England.

William's most trusted regent in Normandy was his wife, Matilda.

Now try this

Describe **one** way in which Norman government relied on the administrative systems that had evolved over many centuries in Anglo-Saxon England.

The sheriff and the forest

Sheriffs had a more significant role in Norman government than in Anglo-Saxon government, and some Norman sheriffs exploited their powers to their own advantage, causing much resentment. Another major focus of English resentment was the royal forest and its laws: the forest became a hated symbol of royal power for ordinary people.

The role of the sheriff

Anglo-Saxon society		Norman society
The king appointed the sheriff to manage the king's land in the earldom. But the earl was much more important than the sheriff.	→	The king appointed the sheriff, who now had much more power: they controlled their shire and answered only to the king.
Sheriffs were responsible for law and order in their shire, answering to the earl.	→	Sheriffs kept this role, with new laws added that punished anti-Norman rebellion.
Sheriffs were responsible for defence of the shire and gathering together the fyrd.	→	Sheriffs kept this role, with new responsibilities as custodian of castles in the shire that belonged to the king.

Why were some sheriffs resented?

- Anglo-Saxon sheriffs were replaced by Normans following Anglo-Saxon resistance (1068–71). Sheriffs had responsibilities for stamping out English rebelliousness.
- Sheriffs took a share of all the revenues they collected for the king. This gave them an incentive to 'squeeze' the locals – the more revenue they got out of the shire, the more the sheriff could keep for himself.
- Sheriffs paid a set sum to manage the king's estates (demesne) and kept any profit the estate made over and above this amount. This also was an incentive to 'squeeze'.
- Sheriffs were involved in many land grabs after the Conquest and their power meant there was very little that victims of their grabs could do to get their land back, unless they had access to the king.

Why was royal forest resented?

- William extended the hunting land he had in his own demesne by taking land away from other landholders and changing it to 'forest': hunting land.
- When land was reclassified as 'forest' it often meant that local people were evicted from the area.
- Forest laws protected quarry (the animals that were hunted), which meant harsh punishments for anyone caught poaching the animals, or who were caught in the forest with tools or dogs that could be used for hunting.
- Forest laws also prohibited damage to the vegetation used by quarry. This meant harsh punishments for people caught cutting wood or clearing land or building houses in the forest.

It undermined William's claim to be just and fair – people suffered just so the king could have deer to hunt.

Made the land grabs of other Normans seem more legitimate – the king grabbed land, too.

Significance of the forest

Harsh punishments (e.g. blinding) for breaking forest laws show the brutal side to Norman rule.

The forest became a source of royal revenue through the fines paid by those caught breaking forest laws and the sale of hunting rights to other nobles.

Now try this

Explain what the introduction of the 'forest' suggests about William's character or personality.

The Domesday Book

The Domesday Book is another example of William's growing power over his conquered kingdom. It was produced as a result of the Domesday survey, ordered by William in December 1085, and told William who held what land and what their obligations were to the king.

The Domesday survey

After a meeting with his advisers at Christmas in 1085, William ordered an investigation of the landholdings of each shire: who held what land, what taxes they owed the king and whether they could pay any more. The results of this survey were written up as the Domesday Book.

There are around two million words in the Domesday Book. Handwriting analysis shows the Domesday Book's records were all written down by one man, almost certainly an Anglo-Saxon because place names and people's names were spelled correctly – Normans tended to spell them incorrectly.

As the work was mostly completed by August 1086, the Domesday Book is a remarkable achievement and shows the efficiency of Anglo-Saxon administration.

Domesday Book facts

- ✓ 13 400 place names are recorded in the Domesday Book.
- ✓ The estimate of England's population being around 2 million in the 1060s comes from analysis of Domesday Book records.
- ✓ The Domesday Book also gives us information about social roles in 11th century England. It lists: 28 235 slaves; 110 000 villeins (peasants bound to their lords through labour service); 14 000 freemen and 24 000 sokemen – a type of ceorl (80% of sokemen were in the Danelaw); 1000 tenants-in-chief and 8000 under-tenants.

Because the Domesday Book doesn't cover the whole area of England, and because it doesn't list whole families, historians have multiplied these figures to produce an estimate for the whole country.

The uses of the Domesday book

The Domesday Book meant the king could see where landholders should be paying more money. It might also have involved ending special tax privileges for tenants-in-chief.

The meeting which decided to carry out the Domesday survey had been called because of the threat of a new Viking invasion in 1085. Although the invasion never happened, it is possible William used the Domesday Book to see how many more knights his tenants could provide for knight service.

Military | Financial | Legal | Financial

The Domesday Book contains records of claims by Anglo-Saxons that Normans had taken their lands. Since the Domesday surveys were made as fairly as possible, with key people from each hundred saying who owned what, the Domesday Book had a role in sorting out legal disputes.

The way the Domesday Book is organised suggests it was a handy guide to working out what reliefs should be charged when land was due to be inherited.

Now try this

Explain **one** way in which the Domesday Book helped William increase his control over England.

The Norman aristocracy

The Normans, as the conquerors and rulers, became the aristocracy in England and influenced language and culture.

Language

Spoken by ruling elite: barons, bishops, knights	Used for all official writing
Norman-French	**Latin**

English	
Spoken by ordinary people, peasants	Written only rarely

 Neither King William nor Archbishop Lanfranc could speak English.

 Writs were written in Latin, not English. Writs in Anglo-Saxon England had often been written in English.

Because Norman nobles had English nurses for their children, many second-generation Normans understood English.

Aristocratic culture

While Anglo-Saxon aristocrats tended to spend their money on rich clothing, jewellery, gifts and lavish parties, the Norman aristocracy tended to put the huge wealth they extracted from England into buildings, especially churches and cathedrals.

Normans showed off their wealth by building very large structures and using innovative and daring, high-impact architectural methods. The arch of this Norman church doorway has been elaborately carved.

Landholding
The Anglo-Saxon tradition was for earls and thegns to pass on their estates to lots of different family members. Norman culture was different. Norman aristocrats tried to pass on their lands to a single heir so that the whole estate stayed together.

Norman culture

Chivalry – the culture of the knight
Chivalry was a complex moral code about how knights should behave. It combined Christianity, showing mercy and the glorification of extreme violence.

The Church and penance
Normans were very religious and believed that they should atone for the violence they had used in conquering England and establishing Norman control over the country. Penance involved prayer and acts that helped the Church, such as building churches or giving rich gifts to the Church. The Normans looked down on the English and their culture. Anglo-Saxon churches were knocked down and many tombs and relics (preserved body parts) of Anglo-Saxon and Celtic saints were destroyed because the Normans did not think they were holy.

Now try this

Identify **two** ways in which Norman noble culture was different from Anglo-Saxon noble culture.

Bishop Odo

Bishop Odo of Bayeux was William's half-brother and a loyal supporter throughout the Conquest. William rewarded him with the earldom of Kent, making him one of England's (and Normandy's) richest men.

The career of Bishop Odo

Timeline

c1036 Odo born. His mother was Herleva, who was also William's mother.

c1049 William makes Odo the Bishop of Bayeux.

1066 Odo contributes 100 ships to William's invasion fleet.
Odo fights at the Battle of Hastings, and is shown rallying panicking troops in a scene in the Bayeux Tapestry.
William rewards Odo lavishly, making him Earl of Kent and many other estates and making him second only to the king in landholdings.

1067 Odo made co-regent of England (with William FitzOsbern) when King William returns to Normandy.

1076 A three-day enquiry is held following complaints to Lanfranc about land seizures by Odo. Odo is forced to return the land.

1082 Odo falls out of favour with William and is imprisoned. He is not released until William's death, after Odo's brother manages to persuade William to show mercy.

1088 Odo leads barons in revolt against William II.

Find out about the revolt on page 30.

The significance of Bishop Odo

William and Odo were half-brothers. William only put his trust in family and a few close friends.

This appointment was significant because Odo's bad reputation would otherwise have kept him out of Church leadership. He was in William's debt.

Odo's contribution to the invasion was significant. William had to reward him, and others like him, with land after England was conquered, which made it difficult to prevent trouble from Anglo-Saxons who had lost land and power. Odo's wealth is an example of how the Conquest rapidly changed the fortunes of some Normans.

Odo commissioned the Bayeux Tapestry as a piece of Norman propaganda, designed to boost the story that William was England's rightful king.

The regency was a disaster for relations between Normans and Anglo-Saxons. The co-regents allowed theft of lands and rape of Anglo-Saxon women. Resentment resulted in Anglo-Saxon resistance.

It is significant that there were limits to what even a Norman like Odo could do, though probably he only got into trouble because he took land from the Church in a way that aggravated Lanfranc.

Likely reasons for William's actions against Odo are mismanagement of his earldom and the claim that Odo tried to take some knights with him to Rome in a bid to become pope. Odo's imprisonment is significant because it shows how William wanted loyalty and obedience above all. Family connections only protected people so far.

Now try this

Explain why William may have been angered by Odo taking knights with him to Rome.

William's personality

Contemporaries described William I as stern, determined and greedy. He had a stormy relationship with his eldest son, Robert.

William's early life

- William was the illegitimate son of Robert, Duke of Normandy. He was only eight years old when his father died, but he had made William his heir.
- William faced numerous assassination attempts as he was growing up.
- As a young adult, William was constantly at war defending his dukedom against rivals.

Contemporary reviews of William

The Anglo-Saxon Chronicle for 1087 calls William 'stern and relentless', a man who imprisoned anyone who might challenge him, even his own half-brother Odo.

William of Malmesbury (c1125) noted King William's greed for money, which he explained as being due to William being constantly anxious about being attacked: if he could not beat his enemies with his knights, he planned to buy them off with gold.

William's good points

- 👍 He was devoted to his wife, Matilda, and was devastated when she died. He trusted Matilda's leadership skills: she was his regent many times in Normandy.
- 👍 He was very religious, founded abbeys and was involved in promoting Church reform with his chosen religious leader, Lanfranc.
- 👍 He wanted to be respected as England's legitimate king: he wasn't happy with being just the Conqueror.

William's bad points

- 👎 William was prepared to use extreme brutality to achieve his aims, and the Harrying of the North shows this better than anything else.

William is reported to have repented of his brutal oppression of the English on his deathbed. A Norman monk, Orderic Vitalis, reported that William had regretted that he had 'become the barbarous murderer of many thousands, both young and old, of that fine race of people' – the English.

William's death

- By 1087 William had become very fat and when he was leading an attack against the French castle and town at Mantes, his horse stumbled, throwing William and causing the internal injuries that (eventually) killed him.
- It took from July until September 1087 for William to die, in great pain. When he did die on 9 September, there was panic, as everyone feared that without William it would be every baron for himself!
- At William's funeral his stone tomb was too small to fit him into. His servants tried to squeeze him in, causing his corpse to burst. Everyone ran from the smell.

The death of William I, 1087

Now try this

Orderic Vitalis said William 'would say and do almost anything, although it was unbecoming to his majesty, where the hope of money enticed him'. Explain **one** reason for William's greed.

Robert Curthose and revolt, 1077–80

William bullied his eldest son, Robert, and refused to let him have any real power in Normandy. This led to open rebellion by Robert from 1077–80, to the extent that he even fought his father in battle at Gerberoy, France.

Robert Curthose

Robert Curthose was William and Matilda's eldest son. He was probably born in 1054.

'Curthose' was a nickname William gave him meaning something like 'shorty' or 'dumpy legs'. William of Malmesbury said he was short, with a protruding belly.

He was a good warrior but William did not think he was ready to lead the Normans against their enemies. Robert was lazy and weak-willed.

Robert had a difficult relationship with his father, but was a favourite of his mother (she had at least nine children to choose from).

Robert Curthose (1054?–1134) is buried in Gloucester Cathedral, with this effigy of him on his tomb.

Robert's revolt

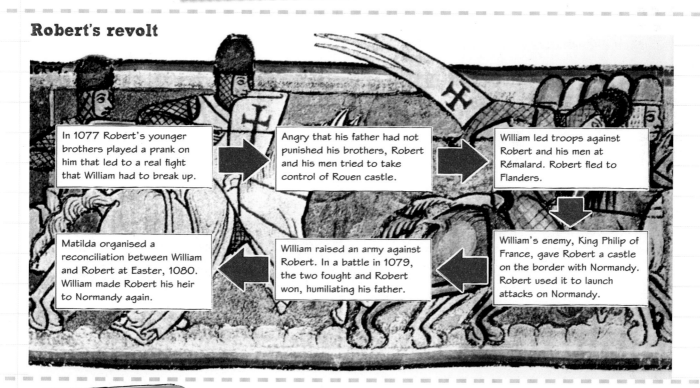

In 1077 Robert's younger brothers played a prank on him that led to a real fight that William had to break up.

Angry that his father had not punished his brothers, Robert and his men tried to take control of Rouen castle.

William led troops against Robert and his men at Rémalard. Robert fled to Flanders.

William's enemy, King Philip of France, gave Robert a castle on the border with Normandy. Robert used it to launch attacks on Normandy.

William raised an army against Robert. In a battle in 1079, the two fought and Robert won, humiliating his father.

Matilda organised a reconciliation between William and Robert at Easter, 1080. William made Robert his heir to Normandy again.

Now try this

Which **two** of the following happened before Robert Curthose's revolt, and which **two** happened after it:

a) William orders the Domesday Book survey

b) the Revolt of the Earls

c) Bishop Odo imprisoned

d) Stigand replaced as Archbishop of Canterbury by Lanfranc?

The defeat of Robert and Odo

The conflicts between William and his eldest son Robert meant William did not want Robert to be king of England, preferring his favourite son William 'Rufus'. However, this was not a situation Robert accepted and there were reasons why some Norman barons did not accept it, either.

Robert was the eldest and the barons had sworn allegiance to him. However, William had his father's deathbed letter to Lanfranc to support his claim.

Norman tradition was that the eldest son inherited all the father's estates.

Robert's conflicts with his father meant his father did not trust him to be king of England.

The disputed succession

William Rufus had a strong character (like his father) which could threaten the power of the barons.

Robert had a weak character and some barons hoped to be able to exploit this.

The barons wanted both Normandy and England to be united under one lord.

Key events of the 1088 rebellion

- In 1087 Odo was released from prison.
- In 1088 Odo led a rebellion against William II in support of Robert.
- The majority of English barons and the English population supported William II.
- Odo and his brother, Robert of Mortain, took refuge in Pevensey Castle.
- Odo then escaped to Rochester castle, waiting for Robert Curthose's support.
- Robert never arrived and Odo was forced to surrender. He was exiled.

Explaining the rebellion

- William Rufus was able to defeat Odo and Robert of Mortain, and the many smaller rebellions across England of 1088, because of the support of most Norman barons, almost all the English bishops and the English population.
- Bishop Wulfstan crushed rebellions in the Marcher earldoms.
- The English fyrd helped defeat Odo and his brother in the south.

Odo's rebellion failed because the support he expected from Robert Curthose and Normandy never came.

Who supported whom in Odo's rebellion?

Robert Curthose (Duke Robert of Normandy)	Bishop Odo of Bayeux	1088		The English population
	Robert of Mortain		William Rufus (King William II)	The majority of Norman barons
Plus another seven Norman barons including Bishop William of Saint-Calais.				All English bishops (except William of Saint-Calais)

Now try this

Explain why many Norman barons would have preferred England and Normandy to have been under one ruler rather than split between the two brothers, Robert and William 'Rufus'.

Exam overview

This page introduces you to the main features and requirements of the Paper 2 Option B1 exam.

About Paper 2

- Paper 2 is for both your period study and your British depth study.
- Anglo-Saxon and Norman England is a British depth study – it will be in Section B of Paper 2: Medieval depth options.
- Anglo-Saxon and Norman England is Option B1. You will see where it starts on the exam paper with a heading like this:

> **Option B1: Anglo-Saxon and Norman England, c1060–88**

> The Paper 2 exam lasts for 1 hour 45 minutes (105 minutes) in total. There are 32 marks for the period study and 32 marks for this depth study, so you should spend about 50 minutes on each.

The three questions

The three questions for Option B1 will always follow this pattern.

Question 4(a)

Describe **two** features of …   **(4 marks)**

> Question 4(a) targets Assessment Objective 1 (AO1): it focuses on describing features.

> Assessment Objective 1 is where you show your knowledge and understanding of the key features and characteristics of Anglo-Saxon and Norman England, 1060–88.

> You can see examples of all three questions on the next six pages, and in the practice questions on pages 38 to 49.

Question 4(b)

Explain why…   **(12 marks)**

Two prompts and your own information

> Question 4(b) targets both AO1 and AO2. It focuses on causation: explaining why something happened.

Question 4(c)

Choice of two questions:
(c) (i) or (c) (ii)

[Statement] How far do you agree?
Explain your answer.   **(16 marks)**

Two prompts and your own information

> You have a choice of two questions for 4(c). These target both AO1 and AO2. You need to make a judgement in this question.

> Assessment Objective 2 is where you explain and analyse key events using historical concepts such as causation, consequence, change, continuity, similarity and difference.

Question 4(a): Describing features 1

Question 4(a) on your exam paper will ask you to 'Describe **two** features of...'. There are 4 marks available for this question: two for each feature you describe.

Worked example

Describe **two** features of knight service.

(4 marks)

Links You can revise knight service on page 19.

What is a feature?

A **feature** is something that is distinctive or characteristic – we can tell one person from another, for example, because of their distinctive facial features. When a question asks for two features of something, think about the special characteristics of that something.

Sample answer

Feature 1
Providing knights to the king, which William imposed to gain greater control on his barons.

Feature 2
The knights had to be equipped and knight service was only for a short time.

This is more of a definition of knight service rather than a feature of knight service.

The student has written an **explanation** of why knight service was imposed. As this is a description question, this explanation is not relevant here.

Two different features have been identified but this answer needs more supporting information.

Don't be tempted to write more than two features – you won't earn extra marks.

Improved answer

Feature 1
Knight service was in exchange for a grant of land. The number of knights that needed to be provided depended on the amount of land that had been granted – usually knight service was levied in units of 10 knights.

Feature 2
Knight service lasted for a maximum of 40 days and knights had to be provided with money by their lord to live on during this time – the king was not responsible for feeding them.

The student has correctly identified a feature of knight service (that it was in exchange for land) and has added good supporting information.

The student has now just picked one feature here and added relevant detail to it in a way that demonstrates their knowledge of the topic and their understanding of how knight service is thought to have worked.

Question 4(a): Describing features 2

Question 4(a) on your exam paper will ask you to 'Describe **two** features of...'. There are 4 marks available for this question: two for each feature you describe.

Worked example

Describe **two** features of the rebellion against William Rufus in 1088.   **(4 marks)**

🔗 **Links** You can revise the rebellion against William II (William Rufus) on page 30.

What does 'describe' mean?

Describe means to give an account of the main characteristics of something. You develop your description with relevant details, but you do not need to include reasons or justifications.

Sample answer

Feature 1
The English helped William Rufus.

Feature 2
Odo escaped from one castle and then went to Rochester castle and waited for Robert Curthose.

This is a correct feature of the rebellion but the answer is rather vague and does not demonstrate enough knowledge.

This does describe events of the rebellion but it needs to be refocused into describing a feature: a special characteristic of the rebellion.

Specific detail has been included – Rochester castle – but more support is needed to back up the description.

Improved answer

Feature 1
Bishop Odo had support from some important Norman barons, especially his brother Robert of Mortain, but most barons, the Church and the English population backed William Rufus.

Feature 2
Odo and Robert of Mortain's use of castles was a key feature of the rebellion. They took refuge in Pevensey Castle but when that was captured, Odo escaped to Rochester castle.

Detail has been added to describe the key feature, which is the extent of support for Odo's rebellion.

This has now been refocused to describe the use of castles as a feature of the rebellion. The student does not explain why castles were used but correctly sticks to a description of this feature.

Question 4(b): Explaining why 1

Question 4(b) on your exam paper is about causation: explaining why. There are 12 marks available for this question and two prompts to help you answer. You must also use information of your own.

Worked example

Explain why castles were important in securing Norman England, 1066–87.

(12 marks)

You may use the following in your answer:

• The Marcher earldoms
• Motte and bailey

You **must** also use information of your own.

What does 'explain' mean?

Explain means saying how or why something happened, backed up with examples or justifications to support the reasons you give. Good ways to get into an explanation are to use sentence starters like, 'One reason for this was...' or 'This was because...'

 **Links** You can revise the reasons for building castles on page 11.

Sample answer

Right from the start of the Norman conquest, castles were a vital part of securing control of England. William's men constructed a castle at Pevensey, where the invasion force landed, and then at Dover. It is estimated that 500 castles were built during William's reign.

The design of Norman castles was important. A motte, a high mound of earth, was constructed and a wooden keep built on top. A wooden palisade was constructed around the bailey, which was an enclosure below the keep. The garrison of the castle lived in the bailey, kept their horses here with a blacksmith and other services.

Many of the Norman castles were built in the Marcher earldoms of Hereford, Shrewsbury and Chester. In fact, the first castles in England were actually built in Herefordshire before the Conquest, by Normans working for Edward the Confessor. The reason for this was to defend the border with Wales. Chepstow castle is an example of a border castle. It was built by William FitzOsbern. It was unusual because it was built of stone rather than wood.

The Normans used castles to dominate an area. The area controlled by a castle was called a castelry and the Norman controlling the area was called a castellan. The castle was a base for launching attacks: knights could ride out to suppress unrest. When castles were built at Warwick and Nottingham during the revolt of Edwin and Morcar (1068), they were very important in suppressing the unrest.

 Compare this answer with an improved version on the next page.

 The first paragraph of the answer is very strong. It relates directly to the question and sets up a clear line of argument.

 The second paragraph follows one of the prompts: motte and bailey castles. The student demonstrates good factual knowledge (AO1), but does not use this knowledge in an explanation (AO2). This section should be **explaining** why the motte and bailey castles were important in securing Norman control.

 The third paragraph picks up the other prompt of the question, the Marcher earldoms. Again, the student demonstrates good factual knowledge but there is only one point at which the student gives any explanation: 'The reason for this was to defend the border with Wales.' This is not enough: details should be used to support the explanation, not the other way round.

 Own information is brought into the final paragraph, which is a real strength to the answer. Although the student begins to provide some explanation, generally they again have not got the balance right between AO1 and AO2.

Question 4(b): Explaining why 2

This page has an improved version of the answer given on the previous page.

Improved answer

Right from the start of the Norman conquest, castles were a vital part of securing control of England. William's men constructed a castle at Pevensey, where the invasion force landed, and then at Dover. It is estimated that 500 castles were built during William's reign.

The motte and bailey design of Norman castles was new in England and the English had no tactics for defeating them. The motte was made of earth (fire-proof) and made attacking the keep very difficult. The bailey sheltered soldiers and mounted troops, so Normans could quickly retreat to safety if needed, and could ride out rapidly to put down unrest. This made Norman castles very effective for controlling an area.

Many of the Norman castles were built in the Marcher earldoms of Hereford, Shrewsbury and Chester in order to defend the border with Wales. Attacks from Wales would put pressure on Norman control of England, especially if the Welsh joined Anglo-Saxon resistance. Castles were located at strategic points along roads, rivers and mountain passes, which enabled them to guard against invasions. Marcher castles were also bases for invasions into Wales.

In the revolt of Edwin and Morcar (1068), William responded to the unrest by building castles in Edwin's earldom of Mercia: at Warwick and Nottingham. As soon as castle construction began, Edwin and Morcar submitted to William. This was because they understood the military power that castles gave the Normans. Once a castle dominated a town, the English there were powerless.

Analysis is about examining something carefully in order to identify the reasons that explain it. The most successful answers to 4(b) questions provide an analytical explanation. This means a tight focus on what the question is asking, and careful selection of reasons that provide a well-thought-through explanation.

Causation questions

Question 4(b) is about causation – causes. These questions have 6 marks for AO1 (accurate and relevant information) and 6 marks for AO2 (explanation and analysis). Strong answers combine explanation and analysis (AO2) with relevant information (AO1).

This first paragraph is not changed as it provides a strong introduction and sets up the student's analysis of the question.

This is an improved version of the answer on the previous page.

The second paragraph is now refocused on explaining why the design of motte and bailey castles was important in securing control of an area. AO1 detail (accurate and relevant information) is still used but is now there to support the explanation.

The third paragraph also now has a focus on **explaining how** castles helped to achieve control: what the threat from Wales was for securing control of England, and how castles were important in meeting that threat.

In the final paragraph, own knowledge is used to give an example of how castles were used in securing control against unrest. Perhaps a bit more time could have been spent on **reasons why** the castles in Warwick and Mercia had such a dramatic effect.

Making a judgement 1

Question 4(c) on your exam paper involves analysing the statement in the question and deciding how far you agree with it. There are 16 marks available for this question and two prompts to help you answer. You must also use information of your own.

Worked example

'The main threat to Norman control of England was Viking invasion.'
How far do you agree? Explain your answer.

(16 marks)

You may use the following in your answer:

- Edwin and Morcar
- The rebellion at Ely, 1070–71

You **must** also use information of your own.

Remember, for question 4(c) you will choose to answer either option (i) or option (ii).

Analysing the statement

Question 4(c) will always include a statement, which may start with phrases such as 'The main reason for...' or 'The main consequence of...' You decide whether you agree or not by considering whether other aspects or reasons, or other consequences, were more important.

Links This question covers Anglo-Saxon resistance on pages 12 and 13, and the Revolt of the Earls, page 17.

Compare this answer with an improved version on the next page.

Sample answer

The threat of Viking invasion was a very great threat to Norman control of England. The rebellions in the north in 1069 involved an enormous force of Danes teaming up with Edgar the Aethling and his supporters to form an Anglo-Danish army that attacked York and killed an estimated 3000 Norman troops. The Danes remained in Lincolnshire as William chased around the country suppressing outbreaks of Anglo-Saxon revolt. This was a threat to William too because the Danes were probably waiting for William's army to weaken.

The rebellion at Ely (1071) also involved a Viking (Danish) invasion. This time the Danish fleet, led by King Sweyn, invaded at Ely and made alliances with local rebel leader Hereward the Wake. With Hereward, the Danes raided Peterborough Abbey, and took a lot of valuable treasure away from Norman control.

The Revolt of the Earls (1075) involved a Viking invasion threat too. A huge fleet of 200 Danish ships arrived to support the revolt in the east of Ralph de Gael, Earl of East Anglia. Even though de Gael's rebellion had not linked up with Roger de Breteuil's revolt in the west, the Danish fleet threatened to give de Gael enough men to overwhelm the Norman defences.

The threat to Norman control from a Viking invasion was the main threat because William was always able to defeat Anglo-Saxon resistance.

This answer demonstrates a strong knowledge of the Viking threat to Norman control of England. It can be difficult to keep the details of the different revolts from getting mixed up, but the student provides a very confident account that selects relevant information and uses it accurately.

One of the prompts provided by the question (The rebellion at Ely) is used but not the other. That is not a problem in itself, as own knowledge of the rebellions in the north and the Revolt of the Earls is used to provide alternative points for discussion.

By this point it is becoming clear that there is not enough **analysis** in the answer. Instead of considering other possible threats to Norman control, or weighing up the seriousness of the threat of Viking invasion, this answer is really only listing Viking invasions.

Although the answer provides plenty of evidence that Viking invasions were a significant threat, it is not until the conclusion that other threats are mentioned. This makes it impossible for the student to back up their conclusion with evidence.

Making a judgement 2

This page has an improved version of the answer to 4(c) (i) on the previous page.

Improved answer

The threat of Viking invasion was a very great threat to Norman control of England. The rebellions in the north in 1069 involved an enormous force of Danes teaming up with Edgar the Aethling and his supporters to form an Anglo-Danish army that attacked York and defeated the Norman defenders. The rebellion at Ely (1071) also involved a Viking (Danish) invasion, as did the the Revolt of the Earls (1075): a fleet of 200 Danish ships intended to invade.

However, how serious was the threat of invasion? Although the Anglo-Danish attack on York in 1069 wiped out an estimated 3000 Norman troops, the Anglo-Danish army then split up rather than face William in battle. In 1071, the Danes again combined with English rebels, but abandoned Hereward once they had the treasure from Peterborough cathedral. In 1075 when the Danish fleet arrived, contemporary reports state that Cnut and Hakon did not dare to fight William in open battle. The Vikings were arguably more interested in taking treasure than in an actual invasion that meant facing up against Norman military might.

So was the main threat to Norman control actually Anglo-Saxon resistance? The revolt of Edwin and Morcar (1068) did not involve the Vikings, and although the revolt fizzled out, it brought together Edwin, Morcar, Edgar Aethling, Waltheof and Gospatric. These Anglo-Saxon aristocrats posed a major threat because of the support of their thegns and the local population and because of Edgar Aethling's legitimate claim to the throne.

In conclusion, the Vikings posed a very serious threat to Norman control, but because the Vikings never seemed prepared to take on William in battle, their threat came from the support they gave to Anglo-Saxon resistance. William recognised that he had to take extraordinary measures (the Harrying of the North, paying the Danes to go away) to prevent the Danish threat. That makes the main threat to Norman control not the Vikings alone, or Anglo-Saxon resistance – either of which William was capable of dealing with. It was the combination of both threats.

The balance of Assessment Objectives

Question 4(c) is worth 16 marks in total. Of this, 6 marks are for AO1 and 10 marks for AO2, which shows the importance of analysis and explanation. AO1 information and understanding also needs to be combined with AO2 for the best results.

Note how the student has now condensed the evidence of the Viking threat into the first paragraph, setting up the analysis which makes up the rest of the answer.

Now the answer considers other factors that may have been important, and also evaluates how significant the Viking threat actually turned out to be.

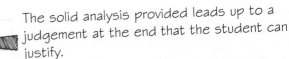

The solid analysis provided leads up to a judgement at the end that the student can justify.

Practice

Put your skills and knowledge into practice with the following questions.

Option B1: Anglo-Saxon and Norman England, c1060–88

Answer Question 4(a), 4(b) and **EITHER** 4(c)(i) **OR** 4(c)(ii).

4 (a) Describe **two** features of the Harrying of the North.

(4 marks)

Feature 1

Guided This was William's destruction of rebel areas in

Yorkshire and other areas of the north in 1069–70 in which

....

....

....

....

....

Feature 2

....

....

....

....

....

....

You have 1 hour 45 minutes for the **whole** of Paper 2, so you should spend about **50 minutes** on this option. Remember to leave 5 minutes or so to check your work when you've finished writing.

Links You can revise the Harrying of the North on page 14.

You need to identify **two** valid features and support each feature.

An example of a suitable feature might be that 'the Harrying of the North involved destroying food stores'. A suitable supporting statement could be 'which the local people and the rebels depended on for food for winter'.

Your exam paper will have a separate space for each feature you need to describe.

'Describe' means you have to give an account of the main characteristic. You do not need to explain why the feature was important or what it was trying to achieve.

Practice

Put your skills and knowledge into practice with the following question.

4 (b) Explain why there was a disputed succession to the English throne when Edward the Confessor died.

(12 marks)

You may use the following in your answer:

- Edward's lack of an heir
- The embassy to Normandy (1064)

You **must** also use information of your own.

....
....
....
....
....
....
....
....
....
....
....
....
....
....
....
....
....
....
....
....
....
....

Remember that question 4(b) is all about causation: this means you are looking for relevant reasons.

For example, you might explain that Harold Godwinson's embassy to Normandy helped lead to a disputed succession **because** William said Harold swore to support William's claim to the English throne in 1064, but then went back on his word in 1066.

Links You can revise the death of Edward the Confessor and the succession crisis on pages 5 and 6.

There are 12 marks on offer for this question. You **must** include your own information to answer the question fully.

Your explanations need to stay focussed on answering the question. Although you might remember lots of detail about Edgar Aethling's claim to the throne, you need to focus on providing **reasons why**, not descriptions of.

Practice

Use this page to continue your answer to question 4(b)

....

....

....

....

....

....

....

....

....

....

....

....

....

....

....

....

....

....

....

....

....

....

....

....

....

....

For example, you might explain that the main **dispute** was between Harold and William. Edward died childless, leaving the succession open, having apparently promised the crown to first William, and then Harold. You might go on to explain that this caused a succession crisis **because**...

Remember: the best answers to Question 4(b) will show a good knowledge of the key features and characteristics of the period **and** analyse causation. They will also show how factors combine with each other to bring about an outcome – so in this case how different factors came together to bring about the outcome of the disputed succession.

Make sure you support your explanation with a good range of accurate and relevant detail throughout your answer.

Practice

Put your skills and knowledge into practice with the following question.

Answer EITHER 4 (c)(i) OR 4 (c)(ii).
EITHER

4 (c) (i) 'The main reason William of Normandy won the
Battle of Hastings was his superior leadership skills.'
How far do you agree? Explain your answer.

(16 marks)

You may use the following in your answer:
- Norman tactics
- The battle of Stamford Bridge.

You **must** also use information of your own.

OR

4 (c) (ii) 'The main consequence of Anglo-Saxon resistance
1068–70 was an increase in Norman control of
England.' How far do you agree?
Explain your answer. **(16 marks)**

You may use the following in your answer:
- The Harrying of the North
- Hereward the Wake.

You **must** also use information of your own.

For **Question 4(c)**, you have a **choice of two questions**. Each question is worth the same number of marks. Although one might immediately seem a question you can answer, do read both carefully to check your choice is the right one.

On the exam paper, the two options for Question 4(c) will be on one page, and you will then turn to the next page to write your answer – like the layout here.

  Links If you decide to answer 4(c) (i), turn to page 42. If you decide to answer 4(c) (ii), turn to page 46.

Links You can revise the Battle of Hastings on pages 8–10. For more about the consequences of Anglo-Saxon resistance in 1068–70, turn to page 12.

Choosing a question

At the top of the first answer page there will be an instruction for you to indicate which of the two questions you have chosen to answer. You do this by making a cross in the box for (c) (i) or (c) (ii). (You can see this on page 42.) Don't worry if you put a cross in the wrong box by mistake. Just put a line through the cross and then put a new cross in the right box.

Practice

Put your skills and knowledge into practice with the following question.

Indicate which question you are answering by marking a cross in the box. If you change your mind, put a line through the box and then indicate your new question with a cross.

Chosen question: 4(c) (i) ☒   4(c) (ii) ☐

Guided   Both sides in the Battle of Hastings were quite

evenly matched: perhaps 6000 men on each side. It was

a very long battle for medieval times: lasting all day. There

were many different factors involved in William's victory, but

in the end it was his leadership skills that ensured his army

beat the Anglo-Saxon army.

....

....

....

....

....

....

....

....

....

....

....

....

....

....

....

....

....

Plan your answer **before** you start writing. List factors that support the statement in the question, and list other factors that go against the statement.

For example:

Support	Against
Invasion needed strong leadership	William was lucky: e.g. storm on crossing
William anticipated surprise attack	Harold's mistakes: e.g. leaving London
Tipped back helmet: rallied troops	General fyrd lacked discipline

Spending a couple of minutes planning your answer means you can write an introduction setting up your arguments.

For each point you make, always then explain how it relates to the question.

Practice

Use this page to continue your answer to question 4(c) (i).

> **Guided** One reason for the English defeat that did not
> depend on William's leadership was that Harold should have
> waited behind the strong defences of London for all his
> fyrd troops to gather. It was a mistake to rush down to
> Hastings because
>
> ....
>
> ....
>
> ....
>
> ....
>
> ....
>
> ....
>
> ....
>
> ....
>
> ....
>
> ....
>
> ....
>
> ....
>
> ....
>
> ....
>
> ....
>
> ....
>
> ....
>
> ....
>
> ....
>
> ....
>
> ....
>
> ....
>
> ....
>
> ....

Remember **only** to answer **either** Question 4(c) (i) **or** Question 4(c) (ii) in the exam.

As with question 4(b), you do not have to use both or either of the two prompts provided by the question. If you do use them, remember that you **must** also include information of your own.

End your answer by saying **how far** you agree with the question statement and give support for your decision.

For example, you might conclude that although Harold's army was understrength and the select fyrd was tired and overconfident from Stamford Bridge, it was William's leadership skills that meant Norman troops and tactics were eventually able to wear down the shield wall and win an outstanding victory.

Practice

Use this page to continue your answer to question 4(c) (i).

....
....
....
....
....
....
....
....
....
....
....
....
....
....
....
....
....
....
....
....
....
....
....
....
....
....

Practice

Use this page to continue your answer to question 4(c) (i).

Practice

Put your skills and knowledge into practice with the following question.

Indicate which question you are answering by marking a cross in the box. If you change your mind, put a line through the box and then indicate your new question with a cross.

Chosen question: 4 (c)(i) ☐   4 (c) (ii) ☒

Guided Immediately after the submission of the earls, William seemed keen to involve Anglo-Saxons in the government of England. Although he reduced the size of earldoms as part of the transfer of lands to his Norman followers, he allowed earls who hadn't fought against him to hold onto earldoms and even proposed a marriage alliance between Earl Edwin and his daughter. However, his reaction to Anglo-Saxon resistance from 1068 saw the rejection of this inclusive approach.

Remember, Question 4(c) gives you a choice of two questions. **In the exam, you only need to answer either 4(c) (i) or 4(c) (ii).**

This question asks about **consequences**: 'The main consequence of Anglo-Saxon resistance 1068–70 was an increase in Norman control of England'. Consequences are the **results** of something. Be careful not to write about 'reasons for' instead of 'results of'.

For example, you might state that one consequence of Edwin and Morcar's rebellion in 1068 was that William built more castles as he marched north, for example, in Warwick and Nottingham. These castles terrified the local people and intimidated the rebels. They were a direct consequence of the rebellion and increased Norman control over England.

Practice

Use this page to continue your answer to question 4(c) (ii).

....

....

....

....

....

....

....

....

....

....

....

....

....

....

....

....

....

....

....

....

....

....

....

....

....

....

....

....

As with question 4(b), you do not have to use both or either of the two prompts provided by the question. If you do use them, remember that you must also include information of your own.

Bring specific facts and details into your answer to show how well you understand the key features and characteristics that are involved in the question.

When you end your answer, make sure you say **how far** you agree with the question statement and give support for your decision.

Practice

Use this page to continue your answer to question 4(c) (ii).

Practice

Use this page to continue your answer to question 4(c) (ii).

....
....
....
....
....
....
....
....
....
....
....
....
....
....
....
....
....
....
....
....
....
....
....
....
....
....
....
....
....

Answers

Where an exemplar answer has been provided, it does not necessarily represent the only correct response. In most cases there are a range of responses that can gain full marks.

SUBJECT CONTENT
Anglo-Saxon England and the Norman Conquest, 1060–66

Anglo-Saxon society

1. The king and the earls

Two from the following:

- Landownership: the king could reward loyalty from his followers by granting them land and, because the king ultimately owned all the land, he had the ability to take land away from those who acted against him. Because land was all-important in Anglo-Saxon society, this gave the king a lot of leverage over other important men.
- Fyrd: when England was regularly attacked by Vikings, the fyrd was organised as a way of calling up a national defence force. It showed the king's power to defend his kingdom: no one else had this power.
- Religion: Anglo-Saxon society was highly religious and people believed that the king was appointed by God. This gave the king a special, holy authority.
- Taxation: because the king decided when the geld tax was levied and because the taxes went to the king, taxation gave him wealth and wealth gave him power. A king who over-taxed his kingdom would not be considered just, however.
- Money: a picture of the king featured on the coins that Anglo-Saxons used, which reinforced his status and image and importance.
- Law-making: the king could decide what was and what wasn't allowed in his kingdom; his role as law-maker also connected with his status as appointed by God and as the protector of his kingdom.

2. Local government and law

Your features could include two from:
- collecting revenues from the king's estates in the shire
- collecting geld tax when this was levied
- collecting fines from the shire court.

3. The economy and social system

Your three reasons could include some of the following:
- Thegns were the warrior class of Anglo-Saxon society: they had the revenue from land-holdings to be able to equip themselves with weapons, armour, a horse and other warrior equipment, and the time to develop fighting skills through training.
- Thegns were important in their local community: they were like 'lords of the manor': their home would have the local church, some defensive capability (a tower) and they would be the landholder that many local peasant workers would rent their land from in return for service to the lord.
- Thegns made up the military core of the fyrd, the 'select fyrd', which meant that they were a vital part of the defence of the kingdom if the king needed them. Thegns would have organised and led the 'general fyrd' men from their area.
- Local priests were mostly employed by thegns, although by the 1060s the Church had started to take control of local priests and to organise them into parishes. Local churches were mostly built by thegns and thegns were therefore important in the religious life of their communities.
- Thegns had a role in the Anglo-Saxon legal system: in some areas, a sort of jury was formed for the shire court by the 12 most important thegns of the shire.
- King's thegns had a higher status than thegns who served bishops or earls or king's thegns: they could take on official duties for the king, like collecting tax from particular areas of the kingdom.

4. The power of the Godwins

A likely answer is: Although Tostig was a southerner he was not from the Danelaw and was without any connections to Northumbria. Waltheof, the son of Earl Siward, was too young to be made Earl of Northumbria: he was only 5 and the north needed a strong leader to defend England against Scotland and to impose King Edward's laws in this 'lawless' part of the Danelaw. Tostig was a strong candidate: he was a good warrior and proven military leader. King Edward relied on the Godwins (and was part of the Godwin family through marriage) and Tostig knew the sort of 'Wessex' law and order that King Edward wanted to see in the north. Tostig's marriage to Judith of Flanders made him very important also, and someone with such important political connections had to be rewarded with an important earldom.

5. Edward the Confessor

Your answer is likely to include some of the following points:

Earl Tostig had been in charge in Northumbria for 10 years when the uprising occurred, and it is likely that the Northumbrian nobility had resented his being in charge for a long time: they would have wanted one of their own to be in charge. Northumbria was in the Danelaw and had been used to being governed independently of England – still part of the kingdom but left to manage its own affairs. The Danelaw had its own laws and customs and had always been taxed only very lightly. So, when Tostig took over and started to impose the laws of southern England in Northumbria, and started to tax the Northumbrians more heavily, this built up long-term resentment. Then Tostig also targeted rivals in the Northumbrian nobility, using his powers as earl to threaten them with arrest for crimes they had not committed if they did not do as he said. The trigger for the rebellion came when Tostig had two of his noble rivals murdered while they were guests in his house. Murder of guests was a horrible crime to the Anglo-Saxons, and it may have been this that made Harold agree with the Northumbrians that Tostig had gone too far. However, there was an additional problem: Tostig was friends with Malcolm III of Scotland and the Northumbrians thought that this meant Tostig did not take the defence of Northumbria against Scottish raiders seriously enough.

6. The rival claimants for the throne

The challenges Harold II faced included:

- Challenges from other powerful Anglo-Saxon earls, especially Wessex's old rival, Mercia.

- Acceptance in the north: would Northumbria accept Tostig's brother as king?

- Tostig: Harold's brother was travelling around Europe looking for allies against Harold, as their father, Godwin, had done against King Edward.

- William of Normandy: reports that William was building an invasion fleet soon reached the king.

Norman invasion
7. Gate Fulford and Stamford Bridge

Your reasons for Harold's victory at Stamford Bridge could include:

- Harold's five-day forced march from south to north was an extraordinary achievement, showing his leadership and organisational skills.

- Harold clearly had support throughout southern England and the midlands: raising an army during harvest time meant communities might struggle to get through winter – it was a huge commitment for the English to make to their new king.

- The Viking army had their weapons and shields with them, but had left their armour on their ships (it was a hot day). Perhaps a third of their men were with the ships, too.

- Harold succeeded in taking Hardrada and Tostig by surprise; they were expecting an exchange of hostages with no expectation that Harold was even in the area.

- Hardrada's army had fought a battle five days before and were not expecting to fight another.

- The Viking troops may have felt misled: they had been informed (by Tostig) that Danelaw England hated its new king so their morale must have been hit when they saw Harold leading a large army against them.

- Harold's housecarls eventually broke the Viking shield wall. This shows that Harold's men had great endurance as well as formidable battle skills.

8. The Battle of Hastings

One advantage of the Norman foot soldiers could include:

- They included archers and crossbowmen, which provided William with a tactical advantage once the shield wall had thinned out.
- William had been able to increase the size of his army by hiring these mercenaries.
- They included heavily armoured warriors who could be effective in combat against the English housecarls.
- The mix of troops gave William more tactical options than the English army had.

One disadvantage of the Norman foot soldiers could include:

- They may not have been trained to fight alongside cavalry, making it more difficult to coordinate troops.
- Some were only lightly armoured, making them weak if caught too close to the English shield wall (e.g. within javelin range).
- Those that were mercenaries needed to be paid and would cause trouble if they weren't.

One advantage of the English fyrd could include:
- Bands within the fyrd would have known each other well, making them more effective as part of the shield wall.
- The select fyrd were trained warriors who knew how to fight in a shield wall and had the same code of honour as the housecarls: to die protecting their lord if necessary.
- The fyrd system enabled Harold to gather more men for his army despite losses of men at Gate Fulford and Stamford Bridge.
- The general fyrd would have included local men, loyal to the Godwins, who also knew the area – this might have helped Harold get control of the hilltop.

One disadvantage of the English fyrd could include:
- The general fyrd was not well trained.
- The general fyrd was not well equipped: most would have had farm implements as weapons, and no armour.
- Although the fyrd would usually have included archers, there seem to have been very few archers in Harold's army. Archers could have been effective shooting downhill at the Normans.
- The general fyrd probably lacked the discipline to stay in the shield wall once it seemed the Normans were running away.
- Once the battle seemed lost, the general fyrd did not have the same code of honour as the select fyrd: they ran for it.

9. William's victory

The feigned retreat was a tactic that William and his knights had used before in battles against the French. It involved a body of troops pretending to flee from the frontline of the battle in a panic, in the hope that some of the enemy would be tempted to run after them. The body of troops could then execute a coordinated move that surrounded their pursuers and cut them down. It is important for explanations of the Norman victory in the Battle of Hastings because some historians believe William used this tactic to trick some of the less disciplined English general fyrd troops to run down the hill after fleeing Normans, who then trapped the English on a small mound at the bottom of the hill and killed them. As a result, the shield wall became weaker; possibly the same tactic was used more than once throughout the 8-hour battle.

William in power: securing the kingdom, 1066–87

William in power

10. Establishing control
- William FitzOsbern was William's first Earl of Hereford. He had been William of Normandy's main cheerleader and fundraiser for the invasion.
- Roger de Montgomery/Roger of Montgomery was William's first Earl of Shrewsbury. He had been William's trusted regent in Normandy during the invasion.
- Hugh d'Avranches/Hugh of Avranches was William's first Earl of Chester. His father had contributed 60 ships to William's invasion fleet.

11. Castles
Two features of motte and bailey castles that made them difficult to attack could include:
- The motte: a steep, high mound that was fireproof (made of earth) and which gave the keep an elevated attack position: archers could fire down from it.
- The keep was protected by palisades and the steep motte, with access up a single flight of steps: this made the keep easier to defend.
- The bailey and keep were protected by a high palisade, often made of two wooden fences with earth rammed in between them, making them less flammable.
- The bailey and keep were sometimes surrounded or partly protected by a ditch, which was sometimes filled with water by diverting a nearby stream or river.
- Access to the bailey was controlled by a gatehouse and was sometimes also protected by a drawbridge, which controlled the entrance into the bailey.
- The bailey palisade often had a walkway along the top, which archers could shoot from.

12. Anglo-Saxon resistance, 1068
When King William returned in triumph to Normandy in 1067 (taking his hostages with him), he left Odo of Bayeux and William FitzOsbern in charge of England as his vice-regents. They did not continue William's policy of trying to achieve a peaceful transfer of power, but instead illegally seized land from Anglo-Saxons and allowed their men to steal and rape without punishment. This was a cause of resentment for the Anglo-Saxon population.

13. Anglo-Saxon resistance, 1069–71
Other outcomes could include:
- Because of discontent amongst his followers about the extent of resistance to the Conquest, William took more land and more money from Anglo-Saxon England (including monasteries and churches) to give his followers more rewards.
- The fact that William was able to get support from other parts of England to put down the rebellions in the north was a significant outcome. It showed that William was accepted as king by some of his new subjects.
- In response to continued Anglo-Saxon resistance, William made changes in landownership that made the right to hold land much more closely associated with service and loyalty to the king.
- Although the Danes seemed to be more interested in raiding than invading/taking on William's army, William remained very concerned about the threat of Viking invasions throughout his life.

14. The Harrying of the North
Previous Viking invasion attempts had often raided up the east coast but had usually made the Humber River and the area around York their main invasion base (as York was an old Viking city and central to the Danelaw). Since King Sweyn changed his invasion base to Ely, in the east of England, in 1070, this suggests that the Harrying of the North had made Yorkshire unsuitable for an invasion base because of the loss of local people who would support a Viking invasion and the destruction of farming in the area, which would have meant there'd be little for the Viking invaders to eat. Achieving this result was likely to have been a reason for carrying out the Harrying of the North.

15. Landownership, 1066–87
Hereward the Wake's rebellion in Ely.

16. Maintaining royal power
William's claim to the throne was that he was the rightful heir of Edward the Confessor, because Edward had promised him the throne and because he was Edward's relation (Edward's mother, Emma, was William's aunt). Harold had sworn an oath to support William's claim to the throne, according to William, which meant that by making himself king he had broken an oath and gone against Edward's original wishes. The consequence for this was that William claimed all the land that had been Edward's was now his, and that all the land that Harold and his brothers had held was forfeited because of their treachery against the rightful king of England. William was then able to use this land to reward his followers, and was able to claim that, as England's rightful king, all the land belonged ultimately to him, as it had done to Edward.

17. The Revolt of the Earls
William would have wanted to reduce the power of his own earls if he suspected that they were becoming too powerful and might challenge him for control of England.

- If earls had too much land, then they might become wealthy enough to challenge him by being able to offer rewards to their own followers to act against the king.
- Although knights were supposed to owe their allegiance to the king, if earls began to gather their own personal armies of knights then this was a major challenge.
- The role that earls had in dispensing justice in their earldoms was a challenge to the king's role as the source of law and peace in the country as a whole. So, William had reasons here to reduce the area that the earl had control over.
- Earls in the Marcher earldoms had the right to build castles without requiring the king's permission first. In Normandy, revolts against William's control depended on castles and control of castles, so it was important to William that castle-building came back into his control, in case earls started to become defensively too strong for the king to defeat them.

18. Features and effects of the Revolt

b) Cutting someone off from the Church community, so they could not confess their sins.

Norman England, 1066–88
Norman England
19. The feudal hierarchy

Your two features could include:
- Knight service: this gave William a large number of trained and equipped knights without the king having to pay for them.
- Knight service also involved tenants-in-chief providing men to garrison the king's castles.
- Tax payments gave William the funds to improve England's defences, for example, with castles or improvements to England's fleet.
- Relief payments increased the royal treasury significantly and this money, like tax, could be used to hire mercenaries for William's wars or to defend England from attack.
- Ceremonies of homage involved men swearing their loyalty to William, which meant he could call upon them to join his wars, along with their followers.

20. The nature of feudalism

Forfeiture: in the event that a land-user did not provide the service required of them, whether military or labour service, they could forfeit (lose) their land. Forfeiture was the punishment for breaking the relationship between the lord and his or her tenant/vassal and was designed to protect the lord's interests.

21. The Church in England

The pope wanted leaders of Churches in England and Normandy and other countries and regions to answer directly to him, as pope and leader of the whole Church. William did not want men in such important and influential positions as archbishops and bishops to have a more important boss than the king, in case that led them to do something in England that the pope wanted but that William did not want, as it would challenge the king's authority.

22. The extent of change

The gradual decline in slavery under the Normans is perhaps the clearest 'not negative' change. In most other areas of society and the economy, the Norman Conquest benefited Normans over Anglo-Saxons. Another possible answer would be: Anglo-Saxon traders who were able to benefit from increased trade with Normandy; although there is not much historical evidence to say whether this happened or not, it certainly could be argued that it was possible.

23. Changes to government

Your answer could include one of the following:
- Norman government used the hide (and the wapentake in the Danelaw) for working out tax obligations, following Anglo-Saxon government practice.
- Norman government kept the Anglo-Saxon shire and hundred as the basis of their economic administration, and also as the basis of community law and order.
- William also seems to have maintained the Witan, or at least a royal council that worked in the same way: important men were invited to join, in order to advise the king on government.
- The Norman economy in England used the Anglo-Saxon system of silver pennies and William kept close control over the royal treasury at Winchester and royal control over the production of the dies used to mint coins, following Anglo-Saxon processes.

24. The sheriff and the forest

Your answer could include the following points:
- The forest was land reserved for hunting, so it suggests that William was keen on hunting. This is confirmed by the contemporary reports that he loved the stags that he hunted as much as if he were their father.
- Some of the forest was land that William had 'inherited' from Edward but he also seized other lands that he wanted to be made forest, too. This suggests that William was greedy, because he already had far more land than Edward had held as king – William's royal estates made up a fifth of all the land in England.
- Although William was keen to portray himself as a just and fair king, the introduction of the forest and the harsh punishments for breaking forest laws makes William look more like a conqueror who took what he wanted, than a king who ruled for the good of his people.

25. The Domesday Book

Your answer could include one of the following:

- The Domesday Book told William what his tenants-in-chief earned from their lands, which helped with controlling them because William could now more easily keep track of what he was owed.
- The Domesday Book was a way of increasing how much money William could extract from his landowners because, as well as assessing what land was currently producing, the surveyors were also looking out for opportunities to increase the revenue that some estates produced.
- It is possible that the Domesday Book enabled William to see where tenants could be providing more knights for knight service to the king. The more knights William had at his disposal, the more military control he had over England and Normandy.
- The Domesday Book helped William work out what reliefs were due when lands were up for inheritance. Reliefs were an important way of keeping Norman nobles under control: low reliefs to reward loyalty, the threat of high reliefs as a warning against any signs of disloyalty. Reliefs also brought in royal revenue, which gave the king more money to spend on control of the country.
- Its role in settling land disputes meant that the Domesday Book had a positive role in William's control of England: sometimes it could reduce resentment against the Normans and give William the respect of his people as a just and wise lawmaker. This would make people happier with William as king: happier people were easier for the Norman government to control.

26. The Norman aristocracy

Your answers could include two of the following:

- While Anglo-Saxon aristocrats spent their money on expensive gifts, rich clothes and banquets yet lived in rather basic halls and houses, Norman aristocrats spent little on entertainment but lived in impressive buildings.
- Norman aristocratic culture was developing chivalry, a set of moral codes and literature about knights. Aristocratic Anglo-Saxons had amazing literature but this was about the loyalty (or disloyalty) of thegns to their lords and their exploits in battles against the Vikings.
- Anglo-Saxon culture used English for both spoken language and much of its official written language, while the Normans spoke Norman French and their official documents (including writs) were written in Latin.
- Norman culture put a high value on a spiritual life for priests, monks and nuns, which meant that they should live separately from ordinary people and devote themselves to holy work. Anglo-Saxon culture in the 11th century did not see this separation as necessary.

27. Bishop Odo

One theory is that knight service was not only a way of giving William the knights he needed without having to pay for them all. It was also a way of ensuring that no rivals developed a private army of knights with which they could challenge the king, either in England or in Normandy. So, if Odo took knights with him to Rome, then it might have angered William because it looked as though Odo was using knights as though they were his private army, not the king's.

28. William's personality

Orderic Vitalis suggested that William's anxiety to get money was due to the king's constant anxiety about being attacked by his enemies. William knew that if he was unable to fight off enemies with his own army, he could use money to buy the enemies off (as he did with the Vikings in 1069–70), or use the money to buy more troops in from Europe (as he is reported to have done in 1085, also against the Vikings).

Other reasons could include the argument that William treated Anglo-Saxon England as a colony, to be stripped of its resources in order to make Normandy richer and richer. Another reason would be that William needed money to buy favour with his supporters and to fund his wars against France.

29. Robert Curthose and revolt, 1077–80

b) and d) happened before the Revolt (the Revolt of the Earls in 1075 and Stigand replaced by Lanfranc in 1071).

a) and c) happened after the Revolt (the Domesday survey was ordered in 1085 and Odo was imprisoned in 1082).

30. The defeat of Robert and Odo

Your explanation could include some or all of the following:

- Having two lords would be difficult for those barons with lands in both Normandy and in England – many of the most important barons were in this position. These men would have to deal with two different administrations, two tax systems and two systems of military obligations.
- The two brothers were likely to fight each other for control of each other's territories. This would mean a clash of allegiance for barons, which might put their landholdings at risk in one territory or the other.
- A war between the two brothers would be sure to mean higher tax levies for the barons and increased demand for knights, both of which would be a financial drain on the barons.
- Norman custom and practice was that the eldest son inherited their father's estate. Barons did not want this to be destabilised because it would put increased strain on their own families and their own inheritance arrangements.

PRACTICE

38. Practice

4(a) For each feature, you get one mark for identifying the feature up to a maximum of two features and one mark for adding supporting information, for example: It was when Normans laid waste to the north (1 mark) which followed the rebellions in the north of 1069 (1 mark).

Your two features could include points and supporting information from the following – yellow highlight indicates features and green highlight indicates supporting information:

- It was the Norman destruction of homes, crops and livestock in northern England in the winter of 1069–70.
- It involved an area stretching from the River Humber to the River Tees, with similar destruction in parts of Staffordshire and Shropshire.
- Norman troops destroyed crops and also seeds for the following year's crops, so that people had nothing to eat and no hope of planting more crops in the future.
- Norman troops killed livestock, which were vital to people's farming, not only for their wool or hides, meat and milk, but because animals pulled ploughs and carts and their manure fertilised fields.
- Norman troops burnt down people's houses, which meant they had nowhere to shelter from the cold winter weather.
- The Harrying of the North is thought to have led to the deaths of as many as 100 000 people, most of whom died of starvation.
- The Harrying of the North caused people to flee the North and look for help in other parts of England.

39. Practice

4(b) There are 6 marks on offer for AO1 and 6 marks for AO2 in this question. If you do not introduce your own information then you can only get a maximum of 8 marks. Your AO1 information needs to be accurate and relevant and your AO2 needs to provide an explanation of the question.

Points that you make in your explanation could include (green highlighting shows supporting information):

- Edward and Edith had no children, which led to a succession crisis because Edward did not have his own 'natural' heir to put forward for the succession.
- Edward had experienced difficulties in his reign, which had led him to agree deals with important people to try and improve his own situation. This helped create the disputed succession crisis because it led to William of Normandy's claim (Edward had asked for his help in dealing with Earl Godwin) and to Edgar Aethling being in England (Edward had brought Edgar and his father back to England from Hungary and made them his heirs).
- The embassy to Normandy in 1064 (or 1065) was when Harold was sent by Edward to Normandy with a message for William. William claimed that Harold swore allegiance to him during this visit and promised to support William's claim to the throne, so when Harold got himself appointed as king as soon as Edward died (on the same day, 6 January), it caused disputes over the succession.
- Harold's fight with Tostig was important in adding to the claimants to the English throne because when Tostig was exiled he went, eventually, to the court of Harald Hardrada and helped convince the Norwegian king to assert his claim to the English throne.
- Another reason for there being a dispute over England's throne was England's relative wealth compared to other European kingdoms and states. This made it a great prize: the king of England was guaranteed great wealth and military power.

41. Practice

4(c) (i) questions have 16 marks on offer: 6 for AO1 and 10 for AO2. Your task is to evaluate the statement and come to a conclusion as to the extent to which you agree with it, justifying your conclusion. This means considering how important the reason given in the statement is compared to other reasons.

You might support the statement with points like the following:

- William's leadership was decisive because he was able to rally his troops at moments of danger for the Normans, for example, when he tipped back his helmet to show he was still alive when his troops were beginning to panic that he had been killed.
- Although Norman tactics were not successful against the English shield wall at first (archers and knights did not weaken the shield wall), William's leadership meant that he was eventually able to find a way to combine his forces to defeat the English.
- The feigned retreat is evidence of very sophisticated leadership tactics. The feigned retreat was responsible for seriously weakening the English shield wall and could have been one of the most important reasons for William winning the Battle of Hastings.

The question talks about 'superior leadership' which means you can talk about ways in which Harold's leadership was not as good as William's leadership, for example:

- Harold's decision to leave London to rush down to engage William in battle so soon after his victory at Stamford Bridge has shown poor leadership if it meant his housecarls would be tired and demotivated.
- Harold's decision to leave London before he had gathered all the fyrd levies may have been inferior leadership if it meant he could have had more troops and, in particular, archers.
- The shield wall depended on discipline and if Harold's leadership over the general fyrd had been better, perhaps the feigned retreat would not have been successful and the shield wall could have held together.

Arguments for other reasons being important could include:

- The battle of Stamford Bridge: Harold's victory against Hardrada and Tostig was a huge achievement but if Harold had not been called north by this unexpected invasion, then the result of the Battle of Hastings might have been very different, if it had taken place at all. Harold's troops would not have been tired, Edwin and Morcar might have been able to send troops to fight William's invasion, and Harold would have been in the south rather than in Yorkshire.

- The shield wall was an old-fashioned tactic compared to the Normans' knights and mixed troops. Medieval warfare continued to refine mounted warfare, suggesting that knights were superior to shield wall housecarls. Rather than William's leadership during the battle, then, the main reason for the Normans' victory could have been their innovative military technology and tactics.

- Luck may have played the main role in William's victory: the two armies were probably pretty evenly matched in terms of numbers; although knights were superior to shield wall tactics, the knights were much less effective when charging up hill. While Norman retreats may have broken up the English shield wall, these might have been real panicked retreats rather than due to William's leadership. If Harold was killed after being shot in the eye with an arrow, then it was probably only luck that meant this happened to Harold rather than to William – the rumour that William had been killed suggests the battlefield was chaotic.

Your conclusion about the extent to which you agree with the statement should then be supported by the arguments you have made: a supported conclusion. For example, if you agreed with the statement your conclusions might start:

- In conclusion, I agree with the argument that it was William's superior leadership skills that meant he won the Battle of Hastings because it was his experimentation with different tactics and troop combinations that eventually broke up the English shield wall.

You should explain why other arguments from your answer did not convince you, for example:

- Although Harold's elite troops were tired from rapid marches and recent battles and Harold had made mistakes in not waiting for all his troops before rushing down to Hastings, Harold was a highly experienced military leader who got the advantage of the hill and was able to construct a highly effective shield wall that held off wave after wave of Norman attacks.

And then add further justification for your conclusion, referring back to points you've made, for example:

- William's leadership meant he had an army that matched the English for size – William had gathered the troops he needed, motivated them, got them to

England and avoided Harold's trap of a surprise attack; his leadership meant the use of knights against a shield wall – something the English had never faced before – and the ability to mix archers, foot soldiers and knights together in coordinated attacks; his leadership may have been behind a feigned retreat that weakened the shield wall and was certainly involved in William rallying his troops when the battle seemed to be going against them.

Avoid introducing new points into your conclusion if you can: the conclusion is where you make your justification for your view of the statement based on the points you've already made.

Note: bullet points have been used in this section to make the points about possible answers clear, but you should not use bullets in your written answers.

46. Practice

4(c) (ii) questions have 16 marks on offer: 6 for AO1 and 10 for AO2. Your task is to evaluate the statement and come to a conclusion as to the extent to which you agree with it, justifying your conclusion. This means considering how important the consequence given in the statement is compared to other consequences.

You might support the statement with points like the following:

- Edwin and Morcar's revolt resulted in castles being built in the midlands and the north, increasing Norman control and triggering the collapse of the revolt.

- The rebellions in the North (1069–70) resulted in the Harrying of the North, which depopulated an important centre of anti-Norman resistance and so increased Norman control of England.

- While William's policy towards the Anglo-Saxon nobility was initially about involving them in governing England, his policy changed by the 1070s, following Anglo-Saxon resistance, which resulted in increases in Norman control through changes in landholding, the feudal system and the Normanisation of the Church and aristocratic culture.

- Hereward the Wake's rebellion at Ely in 1071 was the last Anglo-Saxon rebellion and its failure suggests that Anglo-Saxons from that point on recognised that further resistance only resulted in a ramping up of Norman control.

You might argue against the statement with points like:

- William showed a determination to impose Norman control from the start of the Conquest, laying waste to the area around Dover and fields and villages on the march to London: the Anglo-Saxon resistance came in opposition to Odo and FitzOsbern's open tactics of robbery and rape – that is, Norman control would have increased in England with or without Anglo-Saxon resistance.

- William did not respond to early resistance by earls like Morcar, Edwin, Gospatric or Waltheof by removing them from their earldoms and replacing them with Normans, which would have been an increase in Norman control. Instead, once they had submitted to William again, they were allowed to keep their earldoms.

- Some of the Norman responses to resistance were about guarding against further Viking invasions: it could be argued that the Harrying of the North did not increase Norman control of Yorkshire but that it made a formerly productive part of the kingdom into an economically useless wasteland and may have destabilised other parts of the country due to refugees. However, the Normans must have thought it was worth losing Yorkshire if it meant more security from Viking invasion.

- It could be argued that one of the reasons for the failure of Anglo-Saxon resistance was the acceptance by southern and central England of William as their king. Norman control may therefore have been increased because of the protection the Normans gave these areas from Viking invasions, or because of beliefs that the Normans were God's punishment for England's sins and therefore not to be resisted.

Your conclusion about the extent to which you agree with the statement should then be supported by the arguments you have made: a supported conclusion. For example, if you disagreed with the statement your conclusions might start:

- In conclusion, I do not agree with the argument that the main consequence of Anglo-Saxon resistance 1068–70 was an increase in Norman control of England because the resistance was against a process of Normanisation that was already happening. The increasing Norman control was a consequence of the Normans conquering England.

You should explain why reasons to support the statement did not convince you as much:
- The Harrying of the North did follow Anglo-Saxon resistance but it was a tactic that Normans had used already to impose control without there being any Anglo-Saxon resistance. The Normans had laid waste to towns and villages on the march on London, not because the towns and villages were resisting them, but to impose control. The Harrying of the North was as much about preventing future Viking invasions as it was a response to Anglo-Saxon resistance, and it was not a brilliant way of imposing control because it made Yorkshire into a wasteland that produced nothing of economic value for the Normans anyway.

And then add further justification for your conclusion, for example:
- In much of southern England, it looks as though the Anglo-Saxon population was willing to accept William as king, perhaps because of the protection he offered ordinary people against the threat of Viking invasions. Norman control increased in the south more than it ever did in the north, and did so without Anglo-Saxon resistance. Although Anglo-Saxon aristocrats like Edwin and Morcar rejected the increase of Norman control over their lands, other parts of England accepted it as something that was going to happen no matter what they did.

Avoid introducing new points into your conclusion if you can: the conclusion is where you make your justification for your view of the statement based on the points you've already made.

Note: bullets have been used in this section to make the points about possible answers clear, but you should not use bullets in your written answers.

Notes

Notes

Notes

Notes

Published by Pearson Education Limited, 80 Strand, London, WC2R 0RL.

www.pearsonschoolsandfecolleges.co.uk

Copies of official specifications for all Pearson qualifications may be found on the website: qualifications.pearson.com

Text © Pearson Education Limited 2016

Produced, typeset and illustrated by Tech-Set Ltd, Gateshead

Cover illustration by Eoin Coveney

Picture research by Alison Prior

The right of Rob Bircher to be identified as author of this work has been asserted by him in accordance with the Copyright, Designs and Patents Act 1988.

Content has been included from Kirsty Taylor, Brian Dowse and Victoria Payne

First published 2016

19 18

10 9 8 7 6 5

British Library Cataloguing in Publication Data
A catalogue record for this book is available from the British Library

ISBN 9781292169743

Printed in Slovakia by Neografia

Acknowledgements
The publisher would like to thank the following for their kind permission to reproduce their photographs:

(Key: b-bottom; c-centre; l-left; r-right; t-top)

Alamy Images: Ancient Art & Architecture Collection Ltd 14, Danita Delimont 1, David Hunter 21, Geoff Morgan 05 2, The Art Archive 5, World History Archive 27; Bridgeman Art Library Ltd: Look & Learn 28; Fotolia.com: Vera Kuttelvaserova 24; Getty Images: Angelo Hornak 29t, Dorling Kindersley 11, Geography Photos 26; Mary Evans Picture Library: Interfoto 29b, J. Bedmar / Iberfoto 20, The National Archives, London 25; Robert Harding World Imagery: Walter Rawlings 8

All other images © Pearson Education

Notes from the publisher
1. In order to ensure that this resource offers high-quality support for the associated Pearson qualification, it has been through a review process by the awarding body. This process confirms that this resource fully covers the teaching and learning content of the specification or part of a specification at which it is aimed. It also confirms that it demonstrates an appropriate balance between the development of subject skills, knowledge and understanding, in addition to preparation for assessment.

Endorsement does not cover any guidance on assessment activities or processes (e.g. practice questions or advice on how to answer assessment questions), included in the resource nor does it prescribe any particular approach to the teaching or delivery of a related course.

While the publishers have made every attempt to ensure that advice on the qualification and its assessment is accurate, the official specification and associated assessment guidance materials are the only authoritative source of information and should always be referred to for definitive guidance.

Pearson examiners have not contributed to any sections in this resource relevant to examination papers for which they have responsibility.

Examiners will not use endorsed resources as a source of material for any assessment set by Pearson.

Endorsement of a resource does not mean that the resource is required to achieve this Pearson qualification, nor does it mean that it is the only suitable material available to support the qualification, and any resource lists produced by the awarding body shall include this and other appropriate resources.

2. Pearson has robust editorial processes, including answer and fact checks, to ensure the accuracy of the content in this publication, and every effort is made to ensure this publication is free of errors. We are, however, only human, and occasionally errors do occur. Pearson is not liable for any misunderstandings that arise as a result of errors in this publication, but it is our priority to ensure that the content is accurate. If you spot an error, please do contact us at resourcescorrections@pearson.com so we can make sure it is corrected.